The World Trade Organization

The World Trade Organization

A Citizen's Guide

Second Edition

Steven Shrybman

Copublished by
The Canadian Centre for Policy Alternatives
and James Lorimer & Company Ltd., Publishers
2001

James Lorimer & Company Ltd. acknowledges the support of the Ontario Arts Council for our publishing program. We acknowledge the support of the Government of Canada through the Book Publishing Industry Development Program (BPIDP) for our publishing activities. We acknowledge the support of the Canada Council for the Arts for our publishing program.

Cover design: Kevin O'Reilly

Cover photograph: CP Picture Archive (Joe Brockert)

Canadian Cataloguing in Publication Data

Shrybman, Steven
  The World Trade Organization : a citizen's guide

2nd ed.
Co-published by Canadian Centre for Policy Alternatives.
Includes bibliographical references.
ISBN 1-55028-735-4

1. World Trade Organization. 2. Trade regulation Canada.
3. Foreign trade regulation. 4. International business enterprises.
5. Environmental degradation. I. Canadian Centre for Policy Alternatives. II. Title.

HF1385.S57 2001   382'.92   C00-933056-9

James Lorimer & Company Ltd.,
35 Britain Street
Toronto, Ontario
M5A 1R7

Printed in Canada

Table of Contents

Acknowledgements

I want to thank all those whose courage, commitment and good humour have inspired and sustained the work from which this book has grown. Thanks in particular to: Maude Barlow, Tony Clarke, Bruce Campbell, Mark Ritchie, Scott Sinclair, Ellen Gould, Murray Dobbin, Ken Traynor, Michelle Swenarchuk, Colin Hines, Colleen Fuller, Megan Williams, Jamie Dunn, and Tim Lang.

Thanks also to Charis Wahl, Ed Finn and Kerri-Anne Finn for their valuable help with editing and layout.

Preface to the Second Edition

A Few Good Days for Civil Society (Post-Seattle Update)

On December 1, 1999, millions of people around the world picked up a newspaper or tuned in to their local newscasts to hear about the World Trade Organization for the first time—and the news wasn't reassuring. But the collapse of WTO negotiations, against the backdrop of swirling tear gas, police, national guardsmen in full riot gear, and mass peaceful protests was probably a fitting segue to the next millennium.

Those tumultuous events certainly captured the fundamental challenge of this epoch: the need to reconcile current economic and trade policies with the ecological and social imperatives of civil society. In fact, if left unaddressed, the clash between the "grow now, pay later" paradigm of globalization and the urgent need to confront the challenges of climate change, assuring basic human rights, providing food security for all people, and protecting biodiversity will ultimately be far more explosive than the confrontations that took place on Seattle streets in the waning months of 1999.

In terms of responding to these challenges, the Seattle Ministerial was a bust. No new commitments were made to reconcile trade policy objectives with other societal goals. Most developed countries left Seattle with their commitment to the trade liberalization agenda still very much intact.

But the events surrounding the Seattle Ministerial made it very clear that social justice advocates, trade unionists, environmentalists, and others in civil society will no longer be content to sit on the sidelines while trade rules of the new global ecomomic order are hammered out. For this reason, we should celebrate the events of this WTO meeting as marking a watershed in the evolution of international trade policy and the way trade agreements are negotiated.

While the news coverage focused on the drama on some Seattle streets, the other and largely unreported story of this gathering of WTO members had to do with the tens of thousands of people who attended workshops, teach-ins, peaceful protests, and other events to learn more about the WTO, and express their concerns about the impact of this trade regime on their lives and communities.

The good news is that the Seattle Ministerial represented a turning point in opening the doors to the back rooms of the WTO and other international trade and investment meetings. In the language of international diplomacy, this is the issue of *transparency* and whether it was the protests on the streets or the determined advocacy groups within the meeting rooms, it seems clear that the genie of international trade policy is out of the bottle for good, and for all to see.

This is the second edition of *The World Trade Organization: A Citizen's Guide* and it includes a new section on water in Chapter 6. There is also a new chapter about health and other services that includes an overview of the General Agreement on Trade in Services which is becoming the next focus of debate on the future of trade policy.

Also by way of a preface to this edition, I want to add a comment on the importance of having a rules-based system for international trade. For those who would marginalize the critics of trade liberalization, a particularly effective strategy has been to misrepresent complaints about the WTO as opposition to any international trade agreement or rules-based system of trade.

Let's be clear: we need rules. This is as true for international trade as it is for highway traffic or food safety. The question is not whether we need rules to regulate international commerce and investment but rather what purposes those rules should serve, and who will decide what rules are needed. When it comes to human rights or biodiversity protection for example, most of us would readily concede the need for binding international agreements, even at the cost of national sovereignty.

In the case of basic human rights, universal moral imperatives justify imposing limits on the prerogatives of the nation-state to order its own affairs. In the case of protecting biodiversity and other environmental challenges such as climate change, we are persuaded by the need to ensure our future ecological security. These are global problems that cannot be resolved by the efforts of individual nations alone, but require coordinated and coherent international strategies. Food security for all people and curbing the international arms trade would easily join this list. We might also add rules that seek to address the unequal bargaining power of less developed nations in the world of international commerce.

However, when it comes to the more abstract notions of free trade, the need for binding international agreements is much less clear. Should we cede sovereign national authority in order to create more favourable conditions for foreign investment? Do we need trade rules that seek to limit the capacity of governments to enact regulation for environmental or health protection? Should governments have the power to decide that certain services, such as water treatment and health care, be delivered by the public sector? When trade policies conflict with other societal goals, which should prevail and who should decide? Similarly, when trade rules clash with international commitments concerning human rights or environmental protection, which should take precedence?

We need rules. But those rules must reflect a balance of societal interests, be responsive to the global dimensions of the human and ecological problems looming before us, and be grounded in a fundamental respect for human rights. As this guide reveals, the current WTO framework fails to satisfy any of these prerequisites.

Preface to the First Edition

I recall the first time I encountered the acronym GATT. It was during a casual conversation with a neighbour who worked for the federal government. It was 1982. I said I hadn't heard of it. My neighbour, a trade bureaucrat, was incredulous. How could any reasonably well-educated person not know about something as important as the General Agreement on Tariffs and Trade? I shrugged and said something about trade being outside of my bailiwick as an environmental lawyer. My neighbour looked dismayed.

Looking back on that conversation, it's obvious that my neighbour then understood something that many of us have since also come to recognize. Canada's trading relationships, and the trade agreements to which it has committed, have profound impacts upon a great many aspects of our daily lives. Indeed, we are constantly being reminded of this fact by governments claiming to be powerless to deal with such pressing problems as unemployment, spiraling drug costs, unsustainable natural resources use, declining corporate taxation, or the erosion of Canadian culture. Their hands are tied, they tell us, by the trade deals these same governments have negotiated. These are, obviously, international agreements we should know something about.

Since that conversation with my neighbour 17 years ago, I have learned a lot about Canada's international trade commitments. Indeed, since the advent of the Canada-U.S. Free Trade Agreement a decade ago, many Canadians have been getting a lot of first-hand, and usually unwanted, experience with the impacts of this and other trade agreements on the social, economic, and environmental life of this country.

We have also seen how the enforcement machinery of the North American Free Trade Agreement (NAFTA) and the World Trade Organization (WTO) can be wheeled into action to punish governments that fail to defer to these trade regimes. The list of Canadian public policies, laws, and programs that have fallen—casualties of international trade disputes—includes fisheries conservation regulations, programs to support Canadian publishers, toxic fuel-additive standards, and research and development funding for Canada's high-tech industries. Moreover, the list is likely to grow as current trade challenges to the Auto Pact, water-export controls, film-distribution programs, and supply management for agricultural commodities are decided by international trade tribunals.

But Canada is not only a victim of these trade regimes; it is also using trade dispute processes to challenge progressive initiatives by other governments when it feels they interfere with its trade ambitions. It has joined challenges to U.S. marine conservation laws, initiated a successful complaint against European food-safety regulations, and has recently filed a complaint with the World Trade Organization challenging a ban on asbestos established by the government of France.

As trade rules have come to encompass virtually all spheres of contemporary economic life, there are now few areas of public policy not constrained by these international agreements. Decisions to label genetically modified foods, license generic drugs, or establish public auto insurance are often abandoned long before they come to the point of an international trade dispute. It is this public policy self-censorship, or regulatory chill, that is arguably free trade's most pernicious legacy.

We have also now put the powerful enforcement mechanisms of trade agreements at the disposal of foreign investors who are taking advantage of these new weapons to assail plain packaging regulations for cigarettes; to demand compensation for bans on a toxic fuel additive, freshwater exports, and certain hazardous wastes—all government actions they claim offend their newly-minted investor rights.

This year marked the tenth anniversary of free trade with the U.S. and the authors of this regime gathered in Montreal to proclaim its benefits. Yes, the past decade has been good to some investors and many large corporations. But it has also been a decade of high unemployment, stagnating wages, wholesale job losses, and declining public expenditures on health care, education, the environment, and virtually all public services. While trade with the U.S. has grown, and with it our dependence on this bilateral relationship, much of that growth is attributable to a low Canadian dollar; to the flow of often unprocessed natural resources to manufacturing industries which have more often moved south than north; and to a healthy automobile and auto-parts sector that has nothing to do with free trade but is the product of the Auto Pact—an international trade agreement that represents the antithesis of trade deregulation.

It is not the purpose of this guide, however, to debate the macroeconomic impacts of free trade on Canada. Rather, it is to describe how the rules of international trade have been operating to undermine the capacity of governments to do what most voters elected them to do: develop policy and make laws that reflect the priorities and needs of Canadian society. In the process, we hope to demystify the subject of international trade agreements so that their impacts can be more clearly understood.

To most Canadians, the subject of international trade still remains obscure and esoteric. But remaining uninformed about issues that so directly bear on so many aspects of contemporary life is a luxury no democratic society can afford. It is crucial, therefore, that citizens demand full disclosure and public debate about current and pending international trade agreements. This is particularly important because of the highly secretive way in which these agreements have been negotiated.

The primary focus here is on the World Trade Organization. While much of the WTO agenda has already been established, an important new round of negotiations—styled by its advocates as the Millennium Round—may just be getting under way. An important WTO meeting to be held in Seattle in late 1999 will determine the future course of these negotiations. Whatever the outcome of those talks, it is absolutely certain that international trade agreements will continue to shape economic, social and environmental policy, in this country and others, for decades to come.

So, whether you are concerned about our economy, public health care, the environment, or Canadian culture, some measure of trade literacy will be the price of admission to informed participation in the debate about the future of these crucial policies and programs. The mystique that surrounds present trade-agreement negotiations continues as a serious impediment to this democratic dialogue. Therefore, rather than envisioning trade agreements as arcane documents, think of them as being about the things that matter in everyday life: the food you eat; the work you do (or whether you work at all); the movies, music, and literature you may have a chance to enjoy; the air and water quality in your community; and whether we will continue to have good public schools and universal health care. It is for the purpose of equipping citizens to participate in discussion and debate about these critical public policy issues that this guide was written.

Introduction

1986 was an important year for free trade. It was late that year that leaked copies of draft proposals for a Canada–U.S. Free Trade Agreement began to circulate, and Canadians got their first glimpse into the secretive negotiations that had been taking place between Canada and the U.S. It was also the year that the U.S. tabled a comprehensive set of proposals to overhaul GATT rules that would, if implemented, dramatically enlarge the influence of international trade rules. In the jargon of international trade, the agenda of both initiatives was to "liberalize" international trade by "freeing" it from government regulation.

The underlying premise of this free trade agenda represented a dramatic departure from the trade policies that had guided the economic development strategies of most nations for several decades. These had been founded on the basic notion that governments needed to regulate international trade to ensure that it would serve, rather than overwhelm, the interests of local businesses, workers, and communities.

In support of free trade policies that would abandon these principles, the promise of sustained market-driven growth was offered as the new—and only—path to wealth and economic stability. To achieve this prosperity, governments would only need to allow market forces to operate unfettered by regulation or other government "interference." Today, this agenda is quite familiar: the principles of deregulation, privatization, and free trade have now guided domestic policy for more than a decade.

Unfortunately, our experience with this "grow now, pay later" paradigm shows that it has often been a disaster: for the environment, for workers, for cultural diversity, and for entire populations of developing countries. If measured in terms of wealth distribution, environmental impacts, or economic stability, globalization appears to have exacerbated many of the problems it purported to solve.

If the first article of faith of the free trade paradigm is unregulated growth, the second is specialization. In the parlance of trade theory, this is the principle of "comparative advantage," which posits that all are better off when producers concentrate on what they do best. While this simple notion has a certain appeal, in the real world of mobile capital and concentrated corporate ownership, comparative advantage for nations too readily becomes absolute advantage for corporations as increasingly large and global corporate giants use their size, resources, and mobility to pressure nation states into providing more and more favourable conditions for investment.

To compete, governments often feel compelled to abandon minimum-wage protections, environmental standards, and even corporate taxes to support basic services and infrastructure. Even more problematic are the implications of specialization for economies and ecosystems that are more robust and durable when diversified. Whether expressed as the common sense adage about not putting all our eggs in one basket, or in scientific terms about the importance of biodiversity for the sustainability of life itself, diversity is in many ways the antithesis of the specialization that free trade would have all nations embrace. Indeed, diversity is often seen by the advocates of free trade as an impediment to a truly global economy.

1986 was also an important year for another international initiative—the United Nations Commission on Environment and Development (commonly known as the Brundtland Commission), an unprecedented effort to examine two pressing international problems: global environmental destruction, and poverty and deprivation in many developing countries. A year later, the Brundtland Commission published a chilling assessment of looming ecological crises, and presented various proposals for responding to these threats.

Central to the Commission's recommendations was the call to integrate environmental and economic planning in order to support sustainable forms of economic development. The report underscored the relationship of economic and resource policies to the environmental consequences that flow from them:

It is impossible to separate economic development issues from environment issues; many forms of development erode the environmental resources upon which they must be based, and environment degradation can undermine economic development. Poverty is a major cause and effect of global environmental problems. It is therefore futile to attempt to deal with environmental problems without a broader perspective that encompasses the factors underlying world poverty and international inequality.[1]

But, while the need to integrate environmental and economic planning soon became accepted in theory, only tentative efforts ensued to put this principle into practice. In fact, important national and international "economic" institutions remained largely unaware of, or indifferent to, these policy developments. In virtually all cases, the mandates of these institutions were far too narrow and fragmented to engender any consideration of the ecological dimension of managing economies.[2]

Thus, despite their lip-service to the work of the Brundtland Commission, Canada and other countries made little effort to assess the environmental significance of international trade and trade agreements, and the negotiation of bilateral and multilateral trading agreements remained virtually uninfluenced by the principle of integrating environmental and economic policy.

In many ways, the free trade and sustainable development agendas can be seen as two trains running on parallel tracks. "The Free Trade Express" has continued to gain speed, passing some important milestones along the way: the FTA, NAFTA, several international investment agreements, and finally the WTO. "The Sustainable Development Local," on the other hand, has since been shunted off the main line, getting no further than the adoption of international environmental agreements that lack teeth, and for that reason have been consistently ignored. Indeed, as this Guide documents, the success of free trade has in many ways created dynamics which are fundamentally at odds with those necessary to support any reasonable notion of sustainable development.

The following assessment examines the impact of free trade principles in general, and WTO rules in particular, on a broad spectrum of Canadian policies, legislation, and programs—from the environment to culture. However, because of the pressing nature of the ecological crises before us, an attempt has been made to integrate an environmental perspective throughout. An ecological view of the diverse impacts of free trade on our Canadian society not only reveals common themes, but also suggests the shape of alternatives to the dominant paradigm of unregulated growth and specialized production.

Chapter 1 begins with an overview of international trade and the role that trade agreements play in creating the conditions that support global systems of production and trade. Chapter 2 offers a brief description of the essential elements of the WTO regime—issue-specific trade agreements that deal with everything from food safety regulations to intellectual property rights. This chapter should be helpful for situating the sectoral analyses that follow in the broader WTO framework.

Chapters 3 through 12 examine the many ways in which trade rules have impacted economic, social, and environmental policies, laws, and programs. These look in particular at impacts on global environmental problems; cultural diversity; food security and food safety; natural resource conservation; energy and global warming; environmental standards; patents and other forms of intellectual property; workers; investment; and health care.

Several of these chapters include suggestions for reshaping trade rules to support truly sustainable development. Chapter 13 offers key conclusions drawn from this analysis and suggests a direction for transforming current trade policies so they support, rather than undermine, our efforts to address the social, economic, and environmental imperatives of our time.

The Big Picture

The WTO and International Trade

Rules of trade are embodied in several international agreements. By far the most important of these, historically, was the General Agreement on Tariffs and Trade (GATT), which for decades covered roughly 90% of world trade among nearly 100 countries.

The GATT was initially drafted in 1947 as part of the post-war Bretton Woods Agreements that also established the World Bank and the International Monetary Fund. Since that time the GATT has been periodically amended by complex negotiations that would often span several years. The most recent of these negotiations, known as the Uruguay Round, got underway in 1986 and concluded with the establishment of the World Trade Organization (the WTO) on Jan.1, 1995.

In many ways, the WTO should be seen as the realization of an ambition that took almost five decades to achieve: the establishment of a global trade institution with real authority. During that time other international trade agreements have been negotiated which have often set a benchmark for multilateral agreements such as the WTO. For Canada, the most important of these is the North American Free Trade Agreement (NAFTA), which should be seen as an integral element of a larger trade agenda that is intended ultimately to be incorporated within the WTO.

The Institution

The WTO is located in Geneva, where it is run by a secretariat of approximately 500 trade bureaucrats and officials. However, for reasons we describe below, the influence of this international trade institution far exceeds the relatively modest resources at its disposal.

The WTO is responsible for administering dozens of international trade agreements and declarations which are specific to certain areas of commerce, from agriculture to copyright protection. In addition,

the WTO operates as a forum for trade negotiations, monitors national trade policies and handles trade disputes.

As of March 1998, 135 countries had joined the WTO, and others
had applications pending. However, not all countries belong to the
WTO, China being the most important among them. Several developing countries in Eastern Europe and South-East Asia and Africa
have also yet to gain admission. Membership in the WTO brings with
it access to the markets of other WTO members, the option of
invoking dispute resolution to enforce that right, and the opportunity
to influence the course of future trade negotiations. But these obligations are reciprocal, so countries now seeking membership must
negotiate admission by demonstrating a willingness to open their
markets to all WTO members and to be bound by WTO disciplines.
Thus China's inability to persuade such influential WTO members
as the U.S. of its readiness to embrace the principles of free trade has
so far kept it out of the WTO club.

The WTO is ostensibly run by its member governments—"Parties" in the nomenclature of the WTO. Ministerial Conferences
which represent the penultimate decision-making body of the WTO,
occur every two years as government Ministers gather to discuss
current issues and future directions. Ongoing business is managed by
the WTO secretariat and by officials from the diplomatic missions
many countries maintain in Geneva. The actual day-to-day work of
the WTO is carried out by various committees and working
groups—in the parlance of the WTO, these are General Councils
which deal with such broad issues as trade in goods, services, or
intellectual property, and sub-councils which deal with such specific
issues as textiles, agriculture, and import licensing.

In theory, WTO decisions are "normally taken by consensus."
Voting is also possible by two-thirds or three-quarters majorities with
respect to such issues as new members, amendments to WTO rules,
waivers, and interpretations of WTO Agreements. In reality, however, real decision-making authority at the WTO resides with those
countries with the greatest economic and political clout. This reality
has actually been formalized in the regular meetings of its most
powerful members, the "Quad," which is comprised of the EU, the
U.S., Japan, and Canada. While some developing countries, notably
India and Brazil, have played an active role in dealing with certain
trade issues, the overwhelming majority of WTO members are simply without the resources needed to even assess the implications of

numerous and complex economic and trade policy issues that proliferate in the WTO context.

Thus, notwithstanding a theoretical commitment to democratic process, most developing countries consider the WTO agenda to be the exclusive domain of its wealthiest members. As described by Walden Bello, one of the most informed observers of the WTO: "The problem with transparency and democracy here (in the WTO) is that even within the official process they do not exist.... The Quad countries basically determine which issues are important and come to the floor, and which issues do not come to the floor."[3] According to Bello, current WTO priorities—labour standards, investment and competition policy, government procurement, and information technology—have very little, if anything, to do with the issues of greatest concern to 98% of its members.

The WTO and the Global Economy

While the WTO grew out of the GATT, it should be understood as more revolutionary than evolutionary in its relationship with the trade agreement that preceded it—for several reasons.

First, the world has changed since the GATT was first conceived; we now live in a fully integrated global economy. Transnational corporations control more than one-third of world's productive assets, and their production and distribution systems give little regard to national or regional boundaries. Decisions about locating factories, sourcing materials, processing information, or raising capital are made on a global basis; and a single product may include components from several countries.[4]

This explains why nearly 40% of all international trade takes place *within* corporate families. The growing dimension of global economic integration is also apparent in the rapid growth of international trade itself. To reflect this new reality and consolidate this process of globalization, the WTO codifies the rules upon which these global systems of production and trade depend.

Second, the WTO has extended the reach of trade rules into every sphere of economic, social, and cultural activity. Historically, trade agreements were concerned with the international trade of goods such as manufactured products and commodities. The WTO, however, has extended the ambit of international trade agreements to include investment measures, intellectual property rights, domestic regulations of all kinds, and services—areas of government policy and law that have very little, if anything, to do with trade, per se. It is now difficult to identify an issue of social, cultural, economic, or environmental significance that would not be covered by these new rules of "trade."

But the most important source of WTO authority and influence stems from its powerful enforcement tools that ensure that all governments respect the new limits it places on their authority. Any government found in violation is vulnerable to sanctions too severe for even the wealthiest nation to ignore. For example, in the first trade complaint to be resolved under the WTO, U.S. Clean Air Act regulations were deemed to violate WTO rules. The U.S. was given two options: to either remove the offending provisions of its environmental statute or face retaliatory trade sanctions in the order of $150 million a year.[5]

While previous trade agreements allowed for similar sanctions, they could only be imposed with the consent of all GATT members, including the offending country. WTO rulings, however, are automatically implemented unless blocked by a consensus of WTO members. Moreover, through cross-retaliation, sanctions can be applied to any aspect of the offending country's international trade—in other words, where it will hurt the most.

In the convergence of these factors, the WTO is likely to become the most important international institution ever created.

An Economic Constitution for the Planet

When the Canada–U.S. Free Trade Agreement was concluded, President Reagan described it as the "economic constitution of North America." Soon after the WTO was founded, its Director General, Renato Ruggiero, used similar language to describe the WTO. Like constitutions, trade agreements set out the fundamental rights of their constituents. But these "economic constitutions" have been negotiated behind closed doors with little if any input from any sector other than business. It is not surprising, then, that under the WTO only corporations are the beneficiaries of the rights it creates, and the interests of others in society are nowhere to be found.

A Bill of Rights for Transnational Corporations?

Many have described the WTO's set of rules as nothing less than an international bill of rights for transnational corporations. Consider, for example, the negotiation process that created it.

Because international trade has been considered an arcane subject relevant only to commercial interests, trade negotiations have traditionally been conducted by trade ministers, with no consideration of other societal values.

For example, when the Conservative government of Brian Mulroney was asked what, if any, environmental assessment had been carried out on the impending free trade agreement with the United States, it responded that the trade deal was a commercial agreement and that the subject of the environment had not come up once[6]—an astonishing assessment of an agreement that dealt explicitly with energy, agriculture, environmental standards, forests, and fisheries. Moreover, even as trade negotiations encompassed many more spheres of economic activity, such as services or investment, no meaningful effort was made to include other interested parties in the negotiation process.

Thus, when government consulted on trade matters, it looked exclusively to the business community—i.e., large corporations with a substantial stake in international trade. Trade advisory committees, with very few exceptions, were exclusive clubs for multinational corporations.

Another important norm of trade negotiations is secrecy. Because of their strategic nature, trade negotiations have always been conducted behind closed doors, with little of substance being revealed until negotiations are concluded. Not only is there no public input or accountability, but even many governments—particularly those of developing countries—are left guessing about negotiations that take place almost exclusively among a few key players.

When trade agreements finally emerge, they are presented as an intricate and complex set of strategic compromises that will unravel should amendments be proposed. Thus the normal processes of parliamentary or congressional debate are superseded. Rather, law-makers are presented with a virtual ultimatum: accept the entire package or suffer the consequences of being isolated outside of the global economy. It would be difficult to conceive of a less democratic model for establishing any public policy initiative.

Because of the way trade agreements are negotiated, it is not surprising that the results reflect a myopic preoccupation with the interests of large corporations and a virtual indifference to societal goals such as the environmental protection, democratic processes, workers' rights, or cultural diversity. The WTO can be considered an economic constitution for the planet, yet it was written by—and almost entirely for—the world's largest corporations.

The Agenda: Freeing Corporations from Government Regulation

The essential goal of the WTO is to deregulate international trade. To accomplish this, WTO rules (with one important exception[7]) limit the capacity of governments to regulate international trade or otherwise "interfere" with the activities of large corporations. In fact, WTO agreements are little more than extensive lists of policies, laws, and regulations that governments can no longer establish or maintain.

Some of these agreements prohibit trade measures such as controls on endangered-species trade or bans on tropical-timber imports. Others prohibit regulations that might only indirectly influence trade, such as recycling requirements, magazine content rules, energy-efficiency standards, and food-safety regulations. Still other rules proscribe government measures that have nothing at all to do with trade, such as prohibitions against government regulation of the activities of foreign investors.

The Challenges Ahead

Because the primary goal of free trade is to limit government lawmaking and regulatory authority, serious problems arise for a host of other policy initiatives that depend on such public controls. The establishment of free trade agreements has already created substantial new obstacles to environmental protection, food safety regulation, cultural support programs, and resource conservation initiatives.

If we are to achieve crucial environmental and social goals, the WTO must be transformed into an institution that will foster, rather than undermine, these goals. This will clearly be a difficult challenge, but not unlike the struggle to inform governments and courts about the rights of women and minorities, the entitlements of First Nations, or the importance of environmental protection. The resistance of these institutions to much needed reforms was overcome by informing and then mobilizing public opinion, by fostering social and scientific research, and by persisting in our determination that our governments and courts respond with progressive initiatives. In the process, policy development and law-making were made more open, democratic, and accountable.

The emergence of the WTO will require many of these battles to be fought again, for globalization and free trade are already eroding the hard-won battles of the past three decades. There are, however, two important reasons to be optimistic.

First, the corporate campaign for free trade provides the opportunity to examine a host of environmental, economic, and social issues in their proper context — i.e., as symptoms of profound and systemic problems: unsustainable economic, resource, and trade policies. To use an environmental example: while pesticides, or even a particular pesticide, can become the target of a national environmental campaign, little attention is paid to the agricultural policies that make the continued use of pesticides inevitable. Of course, dealing with the symptoms is important, but we need now to move beyond them to tackle the root causes of these problems. While environmentalists have been shifting the focus of their work and campaigns from symptoms to causes by promoting systemic approaches such as pollution prevention, eco-forestry and organic agriculture, many have yet to seriously consider the economic and resource policies that will be needed to make these goals both realizable and durable. Confronting globalization and deregulated trade will force the development of more sophisticated and structural alternatives to the free trade/free market paradigm.

The second opportunity lies with the need for binding international agreements to confront the the most pressing issues of our times: ecological decline, economic disparities and instability, and human rights. The WTO actually offers a model for such agreements, since it proves that when governments are motivated to do so, they will sign on to international agreements that are effective because they can be enforced by meaningful sanctions. The challenge, of course, is to persuade these same governments to take present economic, social, and environmental imperatives as seriously as they do the interests of their largest trading corporations and foreign investors.

2

The Key Agreements of the World Trade Organization

The WTO is comprised of more than a dozen distinct trade agreements.[8] Among these, and forming the essential platform on which the others are established, is the original General Agreement on Tariffs and Trade (GATT), first negotiated in 1947. Other important agreements include:

The Agreement on Technical Barriers to Trade (TBT);
The Agreement on Agriculture;
The Agreement on Sanitary and Phytosanitary Standards (SPS);
The Agreement on Trade-Related Intellectual Property (TRIPs);
The Agreement on Trade-Related Investment Measures (TRIMs);
The General Agreement on Trade in Services (GATS); and
The Agreement on Dispute Settlement Procedures.

The following offers a summary description of these key elements of the WTO regime. The impact of these trade agreements on a broad range of public policies, from culture to environmental protection, is explored in greater detail in the sector-specific analyses that follow.

GATT 1994

The fundamental infrastructure of the WTO can be found in the GATT, which has been incorporated into the WTO, and where it is described as the GATT 1994 (throughout this text, it is simply referred to as the GATT). For our purposes, the most important provisions of this core trade agreement can be found in three Articles.

National Treatment (NT): Article III

Arguably the most important GATT principle, National Treatment requires all trading parties to treat "like" products of member nations as favourably as its own domestic products. In other words, discriminating between foreign and domestic producers is prohibited.

The sector-specific analyses in Chapters 3–11 illustrate the ways in which this rule has fundamentally undercut the capacity of governments to enact legislation to distinguish among goods that may be identical physically, but have different histories. Thus, under the WTO it is unlawful for governments to discriminate against goods produced or harvested using destructive or unethical processes. Likewise, it is unlawful under these rules for governments to favour goods that are the product of more sustainable or humane systems of production. Chapter 4 (Culture) describes how this rule was enlisted to defeat measures established to support Canadian publishers.

As discussed in some detail under the heading Investment, when national treatment or most favoured nation rules are applied to foreign corporate investment, the result is a disaster for efforts to foster domestic economic development. These rules also essentially abdicate to international market forces the allocation of precious and often non-renewable natural resources.

Most-Favoured Nation Treatment (MFN): Article I

Analogous to National Treatment, the MFN rule requires WTO member countries to treat "like" products from WTO members equally. In other words, discriminating among foreign producers of a given product is prohibited. This rule imposes constraints similar to those arising under National Treatment. It also contradicts key provisions of several international environmental agreements such as the Montreal Protocol on Ozone Depleting Substances, the Basel Convention on Hazardous Waste Trade, and the Convention on International Trade in Endangered Species. These agreements require that less favourable treatment be accorded WTO members if they are not living up to their obligations under these environmental conventions.

A recent WTO case involving banana trade between several Caribbean islands and Europe illustrates that the MFN rule also prohibits the use of special trading relationships to support development-assistance programs to poorer nations. Chapter 9 (Workers) also describes how this principle has been invoked by Japan to challenge the Auto Pact.

Elimination of Quantitative Restrictions (Import and Export Controls): Article XI

Equally far-reaching in its impacts is this prohibition against the use of quantitative controls, such as quotas, embargoes, or bans, on both exports and imports. We will examine in Chapter 6 how this prohibition has been used to attack Canadian export controls on unprocessed resources, such as raw logs and fish, which have historically provided the leverage necessary to force a certain measure of value-added processing to these resources before they are exported. In Chapter 5 we consider the negative impacts of this rule on countries trying to achieve self-reliance in agricultural production, because Article XI also precludes export embargoes on agricultural products even for those nations facing chronic food shortages. In Chapter 3 we describe how this rule also represents a direct challenge to the integrity of international environmental treaties which ban trade in endangered species, restrict the export of hazardous wastes to countries ill-equipped to manage them safely, or which allow countries to ban imports of ozone-depleting substances.

The Agreement on Technical Barriers to Trade (TBT)

It is telling that, in the jargon of international trade law, all environmental, food safety, and other regulatory standards are, *prima facie*, technical barriers to trade. The provisions of the TBT agreement are detailed and complex, but boil down to:

- an international regime for harmonizing environmental and other standards that effectively creates a ceiling but no floor for such regulation, and

- a detailed procedural code for establishing new laws and regulations that is so arduous that it would be difficult for even the wealthiest nations to meet.

When nations fail to observe these new and pervasive constraints on their law-making authority, they are vulnerable to international trade sanctions. It isn't surprising, then, that TBT rules have become important weapons for assailing government regulatory intiatives. Other casualties of these trade rules include U.S. Clean Air Act regulations, marine mammal protection laws, and countless other regulatory initiatives that died of the chill cast by the prospect of international trade disputes. Canada is currently relying upon TBT rules to challenge asbestos regulations in France. Several of the trade cases that illustrate these points are described throughout this guide.

The Agreement on Agriculture

The free trade vision expressed by the WTO Agreement on Agriculture is of an integrated global agricultural economy, in which all countries produce specialized agricultural commodities and supply their food needs by shopping in the global marketplace. Food is grown, not by farmers for local consumers, but by corporations for global markets. The implementation of this global model has already spelled disaster for the food security of poor countries, as subsistence farms are lost to export producers. It is also extremely problematic for environmental and food safety reasons. But these aren't the only adverse environmental consequences of current agricultural trade policies.

The globalization of food production and trade requires that agricultural commodities be transported long distances, and be processed and packaged to survive the journey. In addition to sacrificing quality and variety for durability, this system consumes enormous amounts of energy. When account is taken of all energy inputs, global food production and trade probably consumes more fossil fuel than any other industrial sector. Thus, international agricultural trade policies are likely to cause substantially increased greenhouse-gas emissions and put the imperative of combatting global warming even further out of reach.

Other important aspects of the WTO agenda for agriculture can be found in the agreements on Sanitary and Phytosanitary Standards, and on Intellectual Property Rights. Taken together, these agreements set the stage for the next "green" revolution: the spread of biotechnology in the form of genetically modified foods; terminator genes that prevent seeds from reproducing, so farmers have to buy rather than grow their own seed-stocks; vegetables that are lethal to insects that eat them (at least until whole populations of pests develop immunity); and plants that are virtually immune to pesticides, which therefore can be dosed with pesticides with impunity.

The Agreement on Sanitary and Phytosanitary Measures (SPS)

The provisions of the SPS are very similar to those of the TBT, but deal with laws and regulations regarding food and food safety, including pesticides and genetically modified organisms. Like the TBT rules, the SPS has proven a useful device to undo government regulatory initiatives unpopular with large trading corporations.

Among the first casualties of the SPS was Europe's ban on the importation of beef produced with growth hormones. Another victim of this case was the "precautionary principle," which the WTO held not to be a justifiable basis upon which to establish regulatory controls. Yet the precautionary principle is fundamental to health and environmental protection because it allows action to be taken when the risks warrant, even in the face of scientific uncertainty about the extent and nature of potential impacts.

Another casualty of this WTO Agreement has been efforts to negotiate a "Biosafety Protocol" to the Biodiversity Convention. Various countries, including the U.S., threatened WTO trade action against any protocol that would require a country's prior consent to imports of genetically modified organisms. This WTO agreement also seeks to remove decisions regarding health, food, and safety from national governments and delegate them to international standard-setting bodies such as the Codex Alimantarius, an élite club of scientists located in Geneva. Its location and composition make Codex singularly inaccessible to all but the handful of international corporations and business associations capable of maintaining delegations in Geneva. Not surprisingly, Codex standards often fall substantially short of those established by jurisdictions closer and more responsive to the interests and views of consumers and health advocates.

The Agreement on Trade-Related Intellectual Property Rights (TRIPs)

By conveniently attaching the term "trade-related" as a prefix to its title, this WTO agreement transforms an entire domain of domestic policy and law into one ostensibly suited to WTO regulation. The TRIPs agreement compels all WTO member nations to adopt and implement U.S.-style patent protection regimes. The effect is to provide both U.S. and European transnationals with global patent rights enforceable by retaliatory trade sanctions. Yet the rights of indigenous communities to genetic and biological resources held in common are ignored.

Thus, the appropriation of the global genetic commons by corporate interests is facilitated even to the extent of demanding user fees from the very communities that are the rightful "owners" of the genetic resource. The TRIPs Agreement is also an important impediment to the implementation of the Biodiversity Convention, because of the role it has played in undermining efforts to negotiate a

Biosafety Protocol covering international trade in genetically modified organisms.

A little closer to home has been the impact of this WTO regime on Canadian health care costs, where the federal government has used the TRIPs Agreement as the excuse for reducing opportunities for generic drug licensing. The result has been ever-escalating drug costs at a time when virtually all other health care costs have been declining in response to expenditure cuts made by the same federal government.

The Agreement on Trade-Related Investment Measures (TRIMs)

Like TRIPs, the TRIMs Agreement has a lot more to do with domestic investment policy and law than with international trade. Thus, notwithstanding the characterization of these agreements as "trade-related," they in fact have little, if anything, to do with trade. They do, however, have a great deal to do with asserting the supremacy of international investment in confrontation with virtually any other public policy goal.

The WTO negotiations, however, largely failed to engender the investor-rights regime that the International Chamber of Commerce was championing. Indeed, the TRIMs agreement is only the bare bones of the investment agreement subsequently given full expression in the now-abandoned Multilateral Agreement on Investment (MAI).

But investment will be back on the WTO agenda; and the MAI, and the investment chapter of NAFTA upon which the MAI was based, will provide the template for future WTO investment negotiations. For the objectives of these investment treaties are virtually the same: to open all sectors of a nation's economy to foreign investment; to prevent governments from favouring domestic corporations; to establish the pre-eminence of corporate property rights; and to enable foreign investors to enforce their new rights directly.

It is also significant that key investment rights established under these regimes accrue to the benefit only of corporations that operate multinationally, leaving corporations owned by domestic investors at a distinct disadvantage.

While the investor-rights agenda is constructed on the same platform of National Treatment and Most Favoured Nation treatment common to all WTO Agreements, it goes further, in two critical ways. First, individual investors are allowed virtually unqualified access to international enforcement mechanisms, which may be invoked directly against nation-states. It would be difficult to overstate the implications of this radical departure from the norms of international treaty law, which heretofore had never bestowed rights—with the exception of international human rights—upon individuals, let alone corporations.

In other words, under NAFTA and MAI prototypes, for enforcement purposes, foreign investors are accorded the same status as nation-states.

The second critical departure of the proposed investment regime from the norms of international trade law is to be found under the heading Performance Requirements. These constrain the implementation of domestic investment regulation, even when applied only to domestic investors. Thus, under the rubric of an international treaty, governments would abandon their prerogative to regulate even local investment.

The recent use of NAFTA investor protections by foreign-based corporations to assail toxic-substance regulations, water-export controls, hazardous-waste treatment rules, and even civil court damage provisions, gives a stark indication of what to expect should these investor rights be established globally in the WTO.

The General Agreement on Trade in Services (GATS)

This is yet another WTO Agreement that will often apply to domestic matters that have nothing to do with international trade, per se. The GATS would apply the general GATT principles of Most Favoured Nation and National Treatment to all service sectors. As described on the WTO web-site, the GATS "covers not just cross-border trade, but every possible means of supplying a service, including the right to set up a commercial presence in the export market," which means, for example, setting up a business to deliver health, water, telecommunications, education, or other services. This explains why the WTO also describes the GATS as "the world's first multilateral agreement on investment."

The application of these rules in the areas of health and education would effectively undermine the mechanisms with which Canada has maintained its commitment to public health care and education. For example, national treatment would require governments to provide the same subsidies and funding support to private hospitals and schools as it makes available to non-profit institutions in the public sector. Similarly, the application of GATS rules in the areas of water and sewage services would effectively eliminate the capacity of municipal governments to ensure that these services remained in the public sector.

However, under Part III of the GATS, national treatment and market access rules apply only to those sectors where parties have been willing to make specific commitments. Because the GATS only applies to those service sectors a country volunteers, it is commonly referred to as "bottom-up"—i.e., it applies only when specified. While Canada has so far declined to make wholesale commitments to submit health and education services to the rigours of GATS disciplines, the U.S. and the European Community have both recently served notice of their intention to expand the application of the GATS to these sectors.

The Agreement on Dispute Resolution

Prior to the WTO, trade dispute resolution had been a matter for negotiation and compromise. Trade panels could pass judgment on whether countries were in breach of their obligations; however, compliance ultimately depended on the willingness of each member nation to accept the rulings of trade panels. Under GATT rules, retaliatory trade sanctions could be imposed against an offending nation only with its consent. With the creation of the WTO, the requirement for such consent has been removed, and trade panel rulings are enforceable virtually as soon as they are rendered.

Moreover, enforcement under the WTO involves recourse to the most potent remedies that exist under international law: retaliatory trade sanctions. WTO cases are routinely heard, decided, appealed, and resolved within a year of being brought. It would be impossible to find in any other legal regime, either criminal or civil, sanctions as quick and effective as those provided by the WTO. This effectiveness of enforcement ultimately determines the enormous influence that trade rules will exert over the decisions of governments, even of the world's most powerful trading nations.

Two other features of WTO trade dispute resolution should be noted: it is extremely secretive, and often erratic. Trade disputes are resolved behind closed doors; only national governments have standing to participate; and public interest interventions are not permitted.

It is also significant that trade decisions are not binding on subsequent dispute panels, which are free to ignore the reasoning and findings of previous panels on similar issues. In trade disputes involving environmental or resource issues, trade panel decisions have often been inconsistent and contradictory.

This lack of consistent or predictable interpretation creates great uncertainty for governments now faced with trying to craft public policies and laws that will not run afoul of trade rules. As the trade cases summarized below reveal, would-be regulators are definitely shooting at a moving target, and one that up to this point has been impossible to hit.

However confused the reasoning, a review of WTO rulings reveals two consistent and common themes. The first is the expansive reading given to rules that limit government options that might (even indirectly) interfere with trade. The second is the exceedingly narrow interpretation given trade provisions that might create space for environmental, cultural, or conservation exceptions to the free-trade orthodoxy. This double whammy has shot down virtually every government initiative that has found itself in the cross-hairs of a trade dispute panel. In every case, trade panels have found several grounds on which to rule against the impugned measure, from European food safety regulations to Canadian cultural policies.

Part of the pro-trade bias of these decisions derives from the qualifications of panel members, chosen from a roster of international trade professionals. Nomination to this roster requires no training, experience or expertise in judging complex questions of environmental, social, or cultural policy and law. Moreover, the only parties allowed to participate in trade disputes are national governments, inevitably represented by their trade departments, which tend to share the panel's single-minded and myopic perspective.

With this overview of the key WTO Agreements, it is now possible to examine how these rules for deregulating international trade have actually been put into practice. The following analysis explores how the application of WTO rules has already fundamentally limited the capacity of governments to respond to the enormous social, economic, and ecological challenges that loom ahead.

3

The Global Commons

Although governments remain reluctant to take environmental problems seriously, there is a growing scientific consensus that a devastating global crisis will develop if remedial measures are not taken quickly. This in part explains why, political reluctance notwithstanding, some progress is being made to establish international environmental agreements that provide at least a framework for national initiative.

The most important of these are multilateral environmental agreements (MEAs) that address global warming, ozone depletion, species protection, biodiversity loss, and hazardous waste trade. A small handful of MEAs authorize the use of trade measures, which are central to such goals as banning international trade in endangered species and hazardous-waste. In other cases, trade sanctions are simply the most effective way to ensure that domestic measures are not undercut by jurisdictions willing to ignore international environmental imperatives. However, when the use of such trade measures is considered in the context of WTO rules, several conflicts quickly become apparent.

While no trade dispute has yet challenged actions taken under an MEA, many of the measures that governments must adopt to meet international commitments under such agreements would be unlikely to survive WTO scrutiny. Moreover, unlike NAFTA (Article 104), there is no WTO proviso that insulates these agreements from trade challenge. In fact, the WTO has explicitly rejected proposals by the European Union that measures taken in accordance with international environmental agreements override WTO rules. Moreover, the primacy of trade policy objectives has actually been written into several MEAs.

The Use of Trade Measures to Enforce Multilateral Environmental Agreements

The most important multilateral environmental agreements that use trade provisions to encourage compliance with and implementation of their provisions are:

- **The Convention in International Trade in Endangered Species and Wild Fauna and Flora (CITES).** This convention established regulations based on the vulnerability of a particular species in a specific geographical community. Thus, trade in a particular species may be prohibited in one area and permitted in another.

- **The Montreal Protocol on Substances that Deplete the Ozone Layer (The Montreal Protocol).** This protocol prescribes measures to limit the manufacture of ozone-depleting substances. It also attempts to prevent countries not party to the Protocol from undercutting such measures by prohibiting trade in such substances by signatories with governments that are not signatories to the Protocol.

- **The Basel Convention on the Control of Transboundary Movements of Hazardous Wastes and their Disposal (the Basel Convention).** This convention addresses the fact that many countries that might otherwise be recipients of such transboundary (cross-border) shipments are ill-equipped to manage or dispose of hazardous waste effectively. The counterpart to Basel, the Bamako Convention, prohibits the importation of hazardous wastes into Africa.

When these agreements are considered in conjunction with the prohibitions set out in GATT rules, several contradictions become obvious. First, each of these MEAs seeks to control or ban trade in endangered species, ozone-depleting substances, and hazardous wastes, respectively. Such restrictions, however, are clearly incompatible with GATT Article XI rules disallowing quantitative trade controls.

Second, by authorizing the use of trade sanctions against non-parties to these agreements—including countries that are parties to the WTO—these MEAs allow a form of discrimination that contradicts the Most Favoured Nation (MFN) obligations of GATT Article I. For example, the Montreal Protocol bans trade in ozone-depleting substance with non-parties to the Protocol, but allows such trade with countries that are signatories.

Third, by allowing different rules to be applied to foreign and domestic producers, these agreements also violate the National Treatment requirement set out in Article III of GATT. For example, the CITES Agreement restricts international trade, but doesn't regulate domestic trade or consumption. The same is true of the Basel Convention. Similarly, the Montreal Protocol allows less than national treatment to be given to ozone-depleting substances produced in jurisdictions that are not in full compliance with the Protocol. Thus, all three agreements contradict GATT rules in this way by providing more favourable treatment to domestic goods.

Moreover, the meaning of "like products" in Articles I and III does not allow discrimination against products with the same physical characteristics but very different environmental histories. (This is discussed further in the Tuna-Dolphin case study, later in this chapter). Yet CITES allows discrimination between identical animal or plant products based on whether they originate from a jurisdiction in which the species is threatened. Similarly, the Montreal Protocol discriminates between "like products" based on whether the exporting jurisdiction is a full party to the Protocol.

In other words, free trade provisions force us to ignore different environmental impacts associated with producing goods that may be otherwise identical; lumber from a clear-cut of old-growth forest must be treated identically to lumber from a selective cut of a managed second-growth forest. Thus, it is impossible for consumers and producers to discriminate in favour of sustainable management. In the jargon of international trade, regulations concerning the way products are made are described as production and process methods (PPMs). Trade bureaucrats and adjudicators have been adamant that such measures not interfere with trade, even indirectly.

Given the character and extent of these conflicts, the viability of MEA-based trade measures will depend on whether they are accepted as justifiable exceptions to the trade rules with which they clearly conflict. There is provision made for such exceptions in Article XX of the GATT:

General Exceptions

Subject to the requirement that such measures are not applied in a manner which would constitute a means of arbitrary or unjustifiable discrimination between countries where the same conditions prevail, or a disguised restriction on international trade, nothing in this Agreement shall be construed to prevent the adoption or enforcement by any contracting party of measures:

(b) necessary to protect human, animal or plant life or health;

(g) relating to the conservation of exhaustible natural resources if such measures are made effective in conjunction with restrictions on domestic production or consumption.

A plain reading of these provisions suggests that ample scope for environmental regulation would be possible under Article XX. However, in numerous disputes these provisions have consistently been applied very narrowly. No environmental measure challenged under the GATT, NAFTA, or the WTO has been sustained. While no trade case has specifically impugned a trade measure taken in accordance with an MEA, it is unlikely that such a case would produce a more favourable result.

Two of the first cases to involve Article XX exceptions illustrate some of the problems that arise when this provision has been invoked.

Tuna and Dolphins

During recent years, the trade provisions of U.S. marine mammal protection laws have come under trade fire on several occasions.[9] The first of these such cases (Tuna-Dolphin I) concerned tuna import restrictions authorized by the U.S. Marine Mammal Protection Act (MMPA). These regulated the fishing practices of the U.S. tuna fleet, to limit and ultimately eliminate the "incidental" killing of dolphins. In order to prevent the regulated U.S. fleet from being undercut by foreign producers, the MMPA required the U.S. government to ban the importation of tuna caught by fishing practices lethal to dolphins.

In response to a U.S. environmental group's petition alleging that Mexico and other Latin American countries were ignoring the dolphin protection measures set out by the MMPA, the U.S. imposed an embargo on commercial tuna from these countries. Mexico, which enjoyed a robust tuna-export trade with the U.S., filed a GATT complaint challenging the embargo. Several other countries intervened, among them Canada, which supported Mexico's challenge.

In defense of its environmental regulations, the U.S. maintained that it was not discriminating against Mexican tuna imports, since it treated them in the same way it did the catch of its own fishing fleet. The panel rejected this argument, saying that the MMPA regulations "could not be regarded as being applied to tuna products as such because they would not directly regulate the sale of tuna and could not possibly affect tuna as a product." In other words, the "national treatment" of "like products" required by Article III of the GATT required that no distinction be made among products with the same physical composition or characteristics, however different the processes employed to manufacture or harvest them.

This trade panel also gave a narrow reading of Articles XX (b) and (g) exceptions to the GATT, to preclude measures designed to protect the environment or conserve resources from reaching beyond a country's borders. The panel reasoned that to allow otherwise would be to create a situation in which "each contracting party could unilaterally determine the conservation policies from which other contracting parties could not deviate...." The implication for international environmental treaties or conventions is obvious.

While this aspect of the panel's ruling has been criticized by panels in subsequent disputes, the issue of extraterritorial application of domestic measures remains far from settled.

However, in the second case arising from the same circumstances (Tuna-Dolphin II), a trade challenge was brought by the European Community to a secondary tuna product embargo imposed under the MMPA, which had been established to prevent Mexico and other countries from skirting import controls by simply exporting to the U.S. through countries not subject to the ban.

In that case, the panel could find nothing in the language of GATT Article XX (b) and (g) that would impose such territorial limits. Having opened the door slightly to the potential use of

Article XX exceptions, the panel then quickly closed it again, rejecting the MMPA restrictions "because they required another country to change their policies and practices to be effective." Indeed, by encouraging all countries to pursue global environmental goals, this is precisely what multilateral environmental agreements strive to achieve.

Perhaps the trade panel's most important comment came in its concluding remarks, which focused on fundamental contradictions between the free trade principles of the GATT and trade-restrictive environmental measures. The panel reasoned that, should GATT parties wish to allow such measures, they should amend the GATT to delineate precisely any environmental exceptions to a trade agreement. In other words, if GATT parties wanted trade agreements to accomplish environmental objectives, they should say so.

Unfortunately, making such amendments was flatly rejected during WTO negotiations.

Asserting the Primacy of International Environmental Goals

As the Tuna-Dolphin and other trade cases make clear, current interpretations of GATT rules pose serious problems for international environmental agreements, and are certain to slow efforts to implement existing multilateral commitments. They are also likely to frustrate efforts to develop compliance mechanisms for new environmental conventions and protocols such as the Convention on Biological Diversity (Biodiversity Convention), the Framework Convention on Climate Change (Climate Change Convention) and efforts to conclude an International Convention on Persistent Organic Pollutants (the POPs Protocol).

Implicit in WTO rules—and explicit in trade panel rulings—is the paramountcy of trade policy objectives over environmental goals. This result is not, however, due to any reasoned public policy debate, and few if any countries have encouraged public discussion of the relative priority of environmental and trade policy objectives. Rather, trade and economic departments, which in many ways now dominate all industrialized states, have simply assumed the primacy of their agendas and implemented them. This in turn has further strengthened the influence of these departments over other government spheres.

In fact, the trade bureaucrats and lobbyists have done a much better job of grafting their agenda onto the sustainable development model than environmentalists have done in moderating the "grow now, pay later" model of free trade. For example, Article 12 of the Rio Declaration, negotiated at the "Earth Summit" in Brazil in 1992, states:

The international economy should provide a supportive international climate for achieving environment and development goals by:

(a) promoting sustainable development through trade liberalization.

Mass Extinction Underway, Majority of Biologists Say

A majority of the nation's biologists are convinced that a "mass extinction" of plants and animals is underway that poses a major threat to humans in the next century.... The rapid disappearance of species was ranked as one of the planet's gravest environmental worries, surpassing pollution, global warming and the thinning of the ozone layer, according to the survey of 400 scientists commissioned by New York's American Museum of Natural History. Nearly all attributed the losses to human activity, especially the destruction of plant and animal habitats.
The Washington Post, April 21, 1998

However, there is no empirical proof of the dubious proposition that free trade promotes sustainable development. Moreover, any common ground that does exist between trade and environmental policy goals has been consistently overlooked or ignored by trade panels, which have considered the two to be separate, and often incompatible.

More to the point, given the potentially devastating consequences of global warming, ozone depletion, biodiversity loss, and unregulated waste-trade, it is impossible to accept the proposition that efforts to confront these problems should give way to the blind pursuit of increasing international trade.

While it is possible to read WTO rules liberally enough to accommodate the trade provisions of MEAs, such a reading is exceedingly unlikely—and nowhere in evidence. It is therefore senseless to leave the fate of MEAs to the WTO, especially as there are at least two straightforward ways to assert the priority of the environmental goals engendered by these MEAs.

The first is for MEA signatories to prepare amendments asserting the primacy of MEA provisions in case of conflicts with the rules of trade. To further assure this priority, the WTO should be amended to exempt MEAs from the application of trade disciplines—as is the case under NAFTA.

Trade and the Environment: A History of the Debate

More than ten years ago, Canadian environmentalists were among the first to raise concerns about the relationship between international trade and the environment, during the Canada–U.S. free trade negotiations. They also sounded the alarm that brought these important issues to the attention of environmentalists in the United States, Europe, and elsewhere.

As they predicted, trade dispute processes have become a weapon of choice for attacking environmental and conservation measures in Canada, the U.S, and Europe. Indeed, a GATT challenge to U.S. marine mammal protection legislation focused the attention of U.S. environmentalists and law-makers during the NAFTA debates. Environmental and labour concerns became so troublesome in the U.S. that NAFTA was amended to include nominal environmental concerns.

The most significant of these amendments provided some protection from free trade rules for certain multilateral environmental agreements. The other accommodation to environmental groups, in exchange for their support of NAFTA,[10] was the establishment of the North American Commission on Environmental Cooperation.

The WTO Committee on Trade and the Environment

During the early 1990s, similar developments were taking place in Europe and elsewhere; as well, the environmental implications of Uruguay Round trade negotiations emerged as an important issue. However, environmental concerns never achieved the prominence needed in this larger global context to force amendments to the agreement creating the new WTO. Instead, a long-dormant GATT Committee on Trade and the Environment was reconstituted as the WTO Committee on Trade and the Environment (CTE). The CTE was given a very broad mandate, and in the fall of 1996 reported to the first biennial meeting of the WTO in Singapore.

Few environmentalists knew of its existence, but a handful of environmental groups became actively engaged in its discussions, which ultimately centred on three issues:

1. the relationship between WTO and trade measures authorized by several multilateral environmental agreements (MEAs), such as the Basel Convention, the Montreal Protocol, and CITES;

2. the use of eco-labelling to convey information to the consumer about the product or about the production or harvesting processes associated with that product; and

3. the effects of environmental measures on market access, "considering the benefits of removing trade restrictions."

It is telling that the Committee's discussions had little to do with broadening the scope for environmental initiatives within the WTO. In fact, in important ways, the Committee became a forum for further asserting the paramountcy of trade over environmental policy goals. For example, the Committee has asserted the right of any WTO member to challenge measures adopted by another member, even when those measures are in accordance with a multilateral environmental agreement to which both countries are signatories.

While few anticipated that the Committee's work would actually undermine the integrity of MEAs, this will likely be the effect.

Similarly, in the Committee's discussions on eco-labelling, environmentalists have been put on the defensive to justify eco-labelling schemes intended to inform consumers about the environmental impacts associated with harvesting or production processes.

Unfortunately, the debate on trade and environment has remained at the margins of the WTO; the incremental approach adopted by some environmental groups has yet to yield meaningful gains. At the same time, as the following assessment reveals, trade regimes have emerged as powerful new constraints on environmental law and policy. Moreover, the proliferation of trade disputes concerning environmental, conservation, and public health measures—all of them successful—has underscored the need to develop a much more aggressive agenda for changing WTO rules.

If this goal is to be realized, environmentalists are going to have to play a central role. This will require some measure of trade literacy, for the obscurity of WTO rules is a critical and strategic asset for those promoting the globalization agenda.

4

Culture, Diversity, and Survival

The diversity of cultures within nations and around the world is a major treasure of humankind. The loss of a culture is a significant deprivation for human society. The goal of any cultural policy must be the liberation of the human spirit, and its two fundamental elements must be the twin goals of creativity and access/participation: the right of creators and artists to have opportunities to develop, create, produce, and disseminate their work, and the equal right of the public to the broadest possible opportunities to participate in, be enriched by, and enjoy the arts and cultures of their time and place, their cultural heritage and its living contemporary expressions, and the cultures of other nations.[11]

Free Trade vs. Diversity

In many ways, the struggle against free trade can be seen as resistance to the homogeneity and monopoly control of large corporations in the cause of preserving diversity of all kinds: biological, economic, and cultural. In fact, the need to preserve diversity in all of its forms is a unifying theme that not only informs a critique of globalization but that also describes an essential characteristic of the economic and trade policies that must replace the free trade/free market paradigm.

If we are to establish a truly holistic and sustainable model for human development, cultural diversity must play a fundamental role.[12] Vandana Shiva, one of the most articulate critics of globalization, put it this way:

Diversity is the characteristic of nature and the basis of ecological stability. Diverse ecosystems give rise to diverse life forms, and to diverse cultures. The co-evolution of culture, life forms and habitats has conserved the biological diversity of the planet. Cultural diversity and biological diversity go hand in hand.

We will describe in subsequent chapters how trade and investment rules have been used to defeat efforts to preserve biodiversity or establish diversified resource-based economies. The same trade rules are also being used to bludgeon government programs intended to protect cultural diversity, in the form of domestic film, television, radio, and publishing industries.

Canadian cultural programs have the dubious distinction of being the first to fall victim to WTO rules. Given Canada's long-standing efforts to deal with its particular vulnerability to the hegemony of U.S. culture, it is not surprising that Canada would be the first target of U.S. efforts to promote the interests of its media giants.

For decades, Canada has established policies and programs to foster the development of Canadian culture, and protect it from being overwhelmed by the U.S. film, television, music, and print media that flood across our border every day. To this end, Canada has created such national cultural institutions as the Canadian Broadcasting Corporation, the National Film Board, and the National Arts Centre, and has established clear Canadian cultural mandates for these institutions.

Canada has also created important licensing and regulatory regimes, such as the Canadian Radio-television and Telecommunications Commission (CRTC), which is mandated to regulate the broadcasting, cable, and telecommunications industries to ensure that these serve the interests of Canadians in all parts of the country. In addition, Canadian governments provide direct funding support to Canadian artists and art organizations through the Canada Council, provincial arts councils, Telefilm Canada, and the Department of Canadian Heritage.

Finally, Canada has used various tax and tariff measures to protect Canadian cultural expression. For example, for several decades, under the Income Tax Act, advertising in Canadian magazines was accorded preferential tax treatment. (We will consider this last example in some detail below, in the context of the recent WTO ruling against Canadian efforts to protect domestic magazines.)

However, before we assess how free trade policies undermine the policies, programs, and laws that support our cultural infrastructure, it is important to note the global context within which the assault on cultural diversity is taking place; for Canada is not alone in confronting the tsunami of the U.S.-based corporate media culture that threatens to drown all other forms of cultural expression.

The statistics that follow will hardly come as a surprise to any Canadian,[13] who will know that the "foreign content" referred to is overwhelmingly American. But many Canadians may not know that the pervasive dominance of U.S. culture is being experienced around the world.

For example, for most of this century U.S. films have enjoyed broad international distribution. But the emergence of sophisticated telecommunications technologies and the ascendancy of fully integrated media conglomerates have dramatically accelerated the global reach and penetration of all forms of U.S.-based corporate media.

Foreign content in the Canadian cultural market:

- 70% of the music on Canadian radio stations;
- 60% of all English-language television programming available in Canada;
- 33% of all French-language television programming available in Canada;
- 70% of the Canadian book market;
- 83% of the Canadian newsstand market for magazines;
- 84% of retail sales of sound recordings in Canada (including 69% of French-language retail sales);
- 95% of the feature films screened in Canadian theatres (this percentage is even higher in English-language markets);
- 86% of prime-time English-language drama on Canadian television; and
- 75% of prime-time drama on Canadian French-language television.

In Europe, for example, U.S. films hold 80% of the market.[14] Lost in the transition from domestic to U.S. cinema is the once-proud tradition of such film-makers as Fellini, Bergman, Godard, Bertolucci, Bunuel, Antonioni, Truffault, and Malle—to name but a few. So limited are opportunities for those who would take on the mantle of these brilliant film-makers that a number of contemporary European film producers and directors recently wrote an open letter to Martin Scorsese and Steven Spielberg, pleading for their support for the exemption of films from free trade. They explained their extraordinary letter by saying that they were "only desperately trying to protect European cinema against its complete annihilation."[15]

The U.S. television industry has achieved an even more pervasive universal presence than has film. CNN, which in many countries provides the only available coverage of world affairs, is now broadcast to more than 130 nations. MTV (Much Music to Canadians) dominates television music culture, with an audience far larger than CNN's. As well, there is the appropriation of local television culture by U.S.-based themes. For example, The Price is Right, with its blatant preoccupation with acquisitive consumerism, is watched by hundreds of millions of viewers worldwide: sometimes in English, sometimes dubbed into the local language; and, sometimes as locally produced versions using the same format and themes.

Only in the print media has the influence of U.S.-based corporations been less than universal. Here the global turf has to be shared with consolidated publishing empires presided over by a handful of media tycoons: Rupert Murdoch (Australia and England), Bertelsmann (Germany), Hachette (France), and of course Conrad Black in Canada and Britain.

Exporting U.S. Consumer Culture

It is easy to understand these contemporary realities as a contest between U.S. and other cultures, and in many ways this is precisely what they are. But it is also true that these dynamics represent a struggle between increasingly monolithic media corporations and communities determined to maintain some modest opportunity for their own forms of cultural expression. In fact, concerns about the pernicious influence of large media corporations have also been raised in the U.S. itself. Even *The New York Times* has raised alarm bells about "growing threats to the nation's cultural heritage." But, when President Clinton received the recommendations of the special committee he had established to consider the problem, he evinced little interest in acting on its recommendations to revitalize public and private support for culture in the U.S.[16]

Given the power of the large media corporations, it is not surprising that Clinton had little enthusiasm for trying to hold back the tide of increasingly concentrated corporate control of cultural expression. Not only did his administration do nothing to rein in the power of such media empires as Time-Warner, as the committee recommended, but it actually took up the cudgel on their behalf to assail Canadian programs very much like those advocated by the President's Committee. Foreign trade in telecommunications, film, and other cultural services, where U.S.-based corporations dominate international markets to an extent that far exceeds the global presence of other corporate sectors, is simply far too lucrative to be impeded in any way.

The U.S. balance-of-trade surpluses in cultural products and services are even more important in the context of the enormous trade deficits that the U.S. runs. For example in 1996 U.S. trade deficits of $183 billion were offset by trade surpluses of $74 billion in the area of services.[17]

There are also significant environmental implications that arise from the global influence of U.S.-based media corporations and the consumer-oriented cultural values they purvey. These have to do with the impact of these messages on the hundreds of millions of people in developing countries that are encouraged to strive for the same levels of material consumption they see depicted. When a country, such as the U.S., consumes an enormously disproportionate share of the world's resources, trade deficits would have to be considered an inevitable fact of life.

> "Hollywood is McWorld's story-teller, and it inculcates secularism, passivity, consumerism, vicariousness, impulse-buying, and an accelerated pace of life, not as a result of its overt themes and explicit story-lines, but by virtue of what Hollywood is and how its products are consumed."
> —Benjamin R. Barber

To compensate for these deficits, the U.S. has embarked upon a strategy of exporting U.S. films, television, music, and print media. These cultural products invariably reflect America's unique and highly acquisitive perspective on the world. These messages, both explicit and subliminal, are intended to instill precisely the same unsustainable consumer habits and lifestyles that Americans so enthusiastically embrace. But the ecological imperatives of global warming and biodiversity loss require that we dramatically reduce our rapacious appetite for the world's resources. This is particularly true for developed countries which now collectively consume approximately 80% of global resources. No other country even approaches the enormous rates of U.S. consumption.

If the planet cannot support 300 million Americans consuming at current rates, it certainly won't support the billions more who are being encouraged to strive for the same level of material consumption. The irony, of course, is that in seeking to offset trade deficits—one consequence of its extravagant appetites—the U.S. is promoting the same unsustainable habits that have created its predicament. The globalization of the media and the consumer boosterism embedded in them fundamentally undercuts our capacity to inspire the conservation ethic that is so critical to meeting current environmental challenges.

To ensure that its cultural trade surpluses continue to grow, the U.S. has seized on international trade rules to enforce the continued domination of global markets by U.S. corporations. In the first three years after the advent of the WTO, seven trade cases have been brought concerning cultural products, all but one by the U.S. on behalf of its media giants.

Commercial Goods vs. Cultural Expression

Cultural products and services—art, music, film, and television—are, with few exceptions, subject to the disciplines of international trade and investment agreements. In Chapter II we summarized several of the key structural elements of the WTO; most apply with full force to cultural products (see the periodicals case summarized below). However, there are several other WTO rules that have specific relevance for culture.

GATT Article IV, included at the insistence of the government of France, allows for the imposition of quotas on the import of cinematographic works (film and video). Over time, this definition has been expanded to include quotas on foreign programming in the broadcasting industry as well. In addition, Article XX includes an explicit exception for the protection of "national treasures." This term, however, has been narrowly interpreted to include only works of artistic, architectural, historic, and natural-heritage value. Finally, and of particular relevance, is the General Agreement on Trade in Services (GATS) which covers a wide variety of cultural services, from advertising to telecommunications.

The GATS agreement embraces the basic principles of free trade that impose significant constraints on the policy, program, and regulatory options that might otherwise apply to services. As is true for a growing number of issues that have become the subject of international trade and investment agreements, the services provisions of the GATS often have nothing to do with trade, and everything to do with domestic economic activity and regulatory policy. Commonly described as "bottom-up," the key provisions of the GATS—national treatment and market access—apply only to those sectors with respect to which a country has volunteered these commitments. While Canada has not made any such commitments for cultural services, it must now contend with both U.S. and European Community proposals to greatly strengthen and expand the GATS.[18]

This brings us, finally, to the most noteworthy trade rule concerning matters of culture: the much-vaunted cultural exemption provision of the FTA/NAFTA. Both conservative and liberal federal governments assured us that Canadian culture was safe from free trade rules because it was specifically exempted under these trade agreements.

However, a look at the text of the cultural "exception" clause of the Canada–U.S. Free Trade Agreement [Article 2005], subsequently incorporated within NAFTA [Annex 2106], tells a very different story.

Article 2005: Cultural Industry

1. *Cultural industries are exempt from the provisions of this Agreement, except as specifically provided in Article 401 (Tariff elimination), paragraph 4 of Article 1607 (divestiture of indirect acquisition) and Articles 2006 and 2007 of this Chapter.*

2. ***Notwithstanding any other provision of this Agreement, a party may take measures of equivalent commercial affect*** *in response to actions that would have been inconstant with this Agreement but for Paragraph 1.*

In other words, Canada can maintain and even establish new cultural programs, but the U.S. is free to impose trade sanctions if it does. But wait a minute: doesn't Canada maintain, at least in theory, the sovereign right to legislate? Isn't the whole complaint with free trade that it allows Canada to be punished by trade sanctions for exercising that sovereign prerogative? Finally, wouldn't the whole point of an exemption be to protect Canada from punishing sanctions in order to maintain its legislative and policy options? The answer to each of these questions is, of course, *yes.*

In fact, Article 2005 is merely an exercise in sophistry that offers no effective protection for Canadian culture. It would be a mistake, however, to dismiss this provision as merely ineffectual, since the Article actually may expose Canadian cultural support programs and other measures designed to protect culture to even harsher treatment than would be visited upon other Canadian measures that offend free trade constraints. The phrase "nothwithstanding any other provision of the agreement," in Article 2005.2 arguably allows the U.S. to take measures of "equivalent commercial affect" without going through the consultation and negotiation provisions of NAFTA that apply in other circumstances.[19]

The punitive rather than protective nature of Article 2005 is illuminated in the trade dispute concerning split-run magazines in Canada, which we describe more fully below; but the notion that culture is protected under NAFTA is clearly a deception of grand proportions. The only question left is precisely who was fooling whom. Were Canadian negotiators actually bamboozled by this relatively artless deception? Were their political masters? Or were Canadians deliberately misled by their political leaders in order to quell public protest against a trade regime that Canada was willing to commit to, whatever the cost to Canadian culture sovereignty?

The best way to demonstrate this point is to relate how the rules of trade were used to undermine Canada's ability to support its domestic magazine publishing industry.

Canadian Magazines and Japanese Beer: The WTO Can't Tell Them Apart

In its recent decision on split-run magazines, the WTO's penultimate Appellate Body (the AB) dismissed Canadian magazine safeguards as being in breach of Canada's international trade commitments. In doing so, the AB thought it appropriate to equate Canadian cultural programs with measures Japan had adopted to protect Japanese beer manufacturers—after all a product is a product is a product, it reasoned. However, before we summarize the details of a trade dispute which has been described as "the most dramatic single blow ever leveled against Canadian cultural policy,"[20] let us set the stage.

The domination of Canadian magazine markets by U.S.-based publications is not a recent phenomenon; in fact, it has existed since the first decades of this century. (In 1925, for example, U.S. magazines sold in Canada outnumbered Canadian publications by a margin of 8:1[21]).

And, for just as long, Canadian governments have sought, with varying degrees of determination, to prevent Canadian publications from being entirely swamped in a sea of U.S. print media.

What is a "split-run"?

A "split-run magazine" is a spin-off of a parent publication, designed for a particular regional or niche market. As spin-offs recycle much of the editorial content of the parent, they are relatively inexpensive to produce, so advertising space in the typical split run can be offered at a substantial discount. This is obviously a bargain for advertisers seeking to reach that particular regional or niche market, but a disaster for local publishers competing for those advertising dollars while covering the higher cost of producing original publications.

In the mid-1960s, the Liberal government of the day, firmly committed to strengthening Canadian cultural institutions, established import tariffs under the Customs Act to ensure the viability of at least a small number of Canadian magazines. The tariffs were specifically designed to address the problems created by "split-run" U.S.-based magazines.

In an attempt to level the playing field for Canadian publishers, then Minister of Finance Walter Gordon announced amendments to the Customs Act that effectively imposed an import ban on split-run magazines. To reinforce this prohibition, amendments to the Income Tax Act were also made, prohibiting Canadian companies from deducting the costs of advertising in non-Canadian publications. By all accounts, the measures worked: Canadian publications grew substantially in number and circulation, and the regulations created a truce between U.S. and Canadian publishers that endured for nearly three decades.[22]

This is not to say that U.S. magazines were denied an ongoing and prominent presence in Canada. In 1992–93, for example, U.S. magazine exports to Canada were worth more than $600 million; Canada provided 80% of the foreign market for these publications.[23] However, by the early 1990s, U.S. publications had been consolidated under the control of a handful of very large media corporations. As U.S. media markets had long been saturated, new growth opportunities had to come through global expansion.

This in part explains why one of the world's largest media conglomerates, Time Warner, announced in April 1993 that it would be publishing six "special editions" of *Sports Illustrated* in Canada, electronically transmitting the content from the U.S. to Canada, where it would be printed and distributed. Canadian advertisers in these editions could purchase a full-page ad for roughly half the cost of comparable space in editions prepared for regional U.S. markets.

Faced with a direct challenge to the ban on split-run magazines, the Liberal government scrambled for a response that would allow it to claim some credibility as a defender of Canadian culture. But it had a problem: how to protect Canadian cultural-support programs without straying from the free trade agenda that, suddenly after gaining office, it had become wedded to. The difficulty of reconciling these two agendas is probably the best explanation of why it was not until June 1996 that the government finally responded by tabling Bill C-103, which would impose an 80% excise tax on the gross advertising revenue of split-run magazines.

To counter charges that it was discriminating against U.S. publishers, the excise tax would be applied to magazines distributed outside Canada, including those published by Canadian publishers.

Not unexpectedly, Time Warner took a dim view of the bill, and warned the federal government off its proposed legislation. Indeed, it almost convinced the government to exempt it from the Bill. But, when Bill C-103 was passed unamended, the U.S. government galloped to the rescue of one of its most influential corporate citizens and filed a complaint under the WTO. Casting aside the putative support for Canadian cultural soverignity that it had ostensbily endorsed in NAFTA, the U.S. now invoked the new and much more powerful dispute processes of the WTO to assail not only Bill C-103, but also the Tariff Act provisions covering split-run magazines, which had been on Canada's statute books for decades.

While the WTO would ultimately look like the villain, it should be kept in mind that, but for NAFTA, Canada would have been able to impose a border tax on split-run magazines, however imported or transmitted to Canada.[24] It might also have imposed Canadian-content requirements without risking investor-state litigation that NAFTA alone authorizes. Without discounting the very serious constraints that WTO rules impose on the sovereignty of nation-states wishing to preserve at least small islands of cultural diversity in an increasingly vast sea of corporate and largely U.S.-based culture, it must be pointed out that, at least with regard to culture, NAFTA is far more restrictive of government policy and regulatory options.

Canada, however, rather than adopting measures that would have tested the validity of NAFTA's cultural protection clause, chose a course of action that was likely to land it in difficulties with the WTO. Without access to the behind-the-scenes machinations, it is difficult to discern the government's true motives for choosing the particular approach it adopted. However, it is clear that the government's political exposure around NAFTA and culture is quite high, as is its enthusiasm for extending the NAFTA precedent throughout this hemisphere as part of the Free Trade of the Americas initiative.

Measures Concerning Canadian Periodicals[25]

As noted, the U.S. was the first to enlist the newly-minted dispute resolution processes of the WTO to assert the interests of its media giants. While technical issues were argued,[26] the essential thrust of the U.S. complaint was that Bill C-103 discriminated against U.S. split-run magazines. Canada, it argued, was in breach of WTO obligations to provide "national treatment" to Time Warner products under GATT Article III.

To succeed with its claim, the U.S. would have to persuade the WTO that magazines should be treated like any other goods under WTO rules: a magazine was a magazine regardless of its origin, content or perspective. As the Office of the United States Trade Representative put it, the case had "nothing to do with culture. This is purely a matter of commercial interest."[27]

Of course, Canada protested: surely a magazine's content should be considered a distinguishing feature. A magazine developed specifically for a Canadian readership, published by a Canadian company, and written from a Canadian point of view could not, it argued, be considered "like" one developed in and for another cultural, political, and social context.

To support its case, Canada stressed the importance of advertising revenues to Canadian periodical publishers, and described the direct correlation between circulation, advertising revenue, and editorial content: the larger a magazine's circulation, the more advertising it could attract. With greater advertising revenue, a publisher would be able to spend more on editorial content. The more the publisher spent, the more attractive the magazine would be to its readers, the greater its circulation, and so on. Conversely, the loss of advertising revenue would produce a virtual death spiral: declining editorial content, reduced readership, and a further reduction in the ability to attract advertising.

Not only was the WTO's Appellate Body (AB) unmoved by Canada's arguments, but it actually used them to buttress its conclusion that U.S. and Canadian magazines were in direct competition and therefore "like goods" within the meaning of Article III of the GATT. The AB made repeated reference to earlier trade decisions concerning alcoholic beverages and beer, in which trade panels had dismissed the notion that differential treatment of goods might be justified because of a beverage-particular characteristic.[28] Adopting a purely market-oriented approach to the issues before it, the AB took pains to explain: "The GATT is a commercial agreement, and the WTO is concerned, after all, with markets." Thus, what was true for beer is true for cultural "goods": if they compete, they are alike.

Thus under WTO rules, a newsmagazine is a newsmagazine, regardless of its character, orientation, or national perspective. One can only assume that the same principles would apply to other forms of cultural expression: a newspaper is a newspaper, what difference could national orientation and subject matter make?

Any News Will Do

In rejecting the argument that editorial content is a distinguishing feature of periodical publications, the WTO ignored the significance of the full play of diverse opinions in democratic societies. Ironically, coverage of the split-run magazine imbroglio makes that very case. Our Internet search for articles covering this long-drawn-out struggle revealed that, beginning in January of 1997, Maclean's published 10 substantial articles on the subject. During the same period, we found only one in Time Warner's split-run edition of Time Canada: an editorial denouncing Bill C-55 as "draconian legislation [that] cannot fail to have a chilling effect on press freedom."

The irony that this defence of press freedom was being advanced by the corporation that had motivated a trade dispute to effectively deny Canadians the freedom to hear their own views (on controversies such as the split-run magazine debate) should not be lost.

As is true for the other AB decisions summarized here, this court of last appeal under the WTO has demonstrated a stunning ability to keep its focus on trade policy objectives, no matter how skewed its reasoning might appear in the larger view. Moreover, by so clearly treating magazines as tradeable commodities rather than forms of cultural expression, the WTO also set the stage for further trade challenges to other forms of cultural protection.

It is not necessary to delve into the esoterica of trade dispute resolution to appreciate what this case was actually about. Or perhaps, more appropriately, what it *wasn't* about. The periodicals dispute was not about restricting the access of U.S. magazines to Canadian markets. Nor was it about restricting the circulation of U.S. publications in Canada. Rather, the Canadian measures that so offended Time Warner and the U.S. administration were the modest efforts of our federal government to ensure that Canadians had some opportunity to buy magazines that articulated a Canadian perspective, that reflected Canadian views, values, and sensibilities.

Thus, 75 years after Canada first adopted measures to protect Canadian magazines, the federal government did not (or could not) prevent what it had repeatedly promised would never occur: the sacrifice of Canadian cultural programs on the altar of free trade.

But why? Was this really so that one of the world's most powerful media corporations could add a few points to the circulation figures of one of its dozens of publications? Or was it because the U.S. saw in this dispute with Canada an opportunity to send a message to other WTO members that resistance to the dominance of its cultural products was futile? Indeed, the price of doing so would represent more than the considerable costs of international trade dispute resolution; there would also be the political embarassment of publicly abandoning programs that enjoy strong public support.

Bill C-55

Facing the demise of the Canadian magazine publishing industry as a result of this trade ruling, it was back to the drawing board for Canada, but now with its options considerably narrowed by the WTO. The result—Bill C-55—abandoned Canada's traditional approach of using tariff measures to protect Canadian magazines and instead resorted to criminal law to prohibit U.S. magazines from offering advertising space to Canadian advertisers on pain of reasonably significant sanctions.

Predictably, the U.S. responded quickly; but this time not by invoking the trade dispute resolution processes of the WTO. Rather, having lost its patience with Canadian foot-dragging, it resorted to the far more coercive options available under the very provisions of NAFTA that ostensibly had been negotiated to protect Canadian culture.

The U.S. announced that, should Canada proceed with its proposed legislation, it would immediately impose trade sanctions against a wide variety of Canadian exports, in the amount of $300 million. It chose its targets strategically and in a manner designed to maximize political pressure on the government. In no time, these bullying tactics produced the desired result. One of the first Liberals to break ranks and speak out against the bill represented a riding next to that of Sheila Copps, the Minister responsible for the Bill. Both ridings were dependent on Canada's steel industry and its capacity to export to the United States; steel products topped the list of Canadian exports that the U.S. would impose retaliatory tariffs on. Their constituents couldn't understand why industrial jobs were being sacrificed in order to protect Canadian magazines, and the Minister was hard-pressed to explain.

Notwithstanding its insistence that U.S. threats were illegal under the WTO, Canada quickly capitulated to U.S. demands that it abandon the essence of Bill C-55. Not only would Canada allow U.S. magazines access to Canadian advertising markets, but the federal government actually also agreed to relax Canadian ownership requirements for Canadian magazines!

The only hint as to why Canadian negotiators thought it necessary to offer such a dramatic concession was offered by an unnamed federal official who explained, "They can always hurt us more than we can possibly dream of hurting them,"[29] neglecting to add that this is particularly true now that we have given them the weapons to do so under NAFTA and WTO rules.

Turning the Corner

One might be forgiven for taking from the sad fate of Canadian magazine protection measures a gloomy assessment of Canada's prospects for protecting its culture. But there is good reason to be hopeful that we may have just turned a corner that will enable Canada and other countries to regain some the ground that WTO rules have taken away. The critical moment that may have signalled this about-face came with the recent defeat of the Multilateral Agreement on Investment, discussed in detail in Chapter XI, when the Government of France formally withdrew from OECD negotiations. Prominent among its reasons for doing so were concerns about the potential impact of this investment treaty on its ability to protect French culture.[30]

Canada and France have worked closely in seeking ways to preserve their prerogatives to protect their own forms of cultural expression. Although Canada was an ardent supporter of the MAI, it should
feel emboldened by France's actions to more determinedly resist
U.S. demands about Canadian cultural programs. The efforts of Canada's Minister of Culture, Sheila Copps, to build international support for exempting culture from free trade disciplines is an important
step in this direction.

We began the chapter by quoting from the report of an important
international forum of cultural non-governmental organizations that
met in Ottawa in 1998. In addition to describing the importance of
cultural diversity to our human community, the conference also
mapped out a strategy for pushing back against the aggressive assault
of U.S.-based corporate media culture.

Recognizing that human beings live not only in distinct, diverse
national and cultural contexts, but also in a world in which nations
and cultures are increasingly interdependent, this meeting had as its
goal the development of opportunities for international cooperation
among cultural NGOs:

- to preserve, enhance and nurture cultural pluralism and cultural
  diversity;

- to support efforts to ensure that international trade agreements
  recognize and respect distinctive national and local cultures;
  and

- to encourage the inclusion of cultural issues in development
  policies and to foster an increased role for culture in international relations.

The defeat of Canadian magazine protections should not be a
cause for resignation, but for more determined efforts to insist that
Canada honour its commitment to protect our culture by working
with its allies to transform WTO rules to support, rather than undermine, the diversity that is fundamental to life itself.

As David Suzuki puts it:

Nature is in constant flux, and diversity is key to survival. If
change is inevitable but unpredictable, then the best tactic for
survival is to act in ways that retain the most diversity; then,

when circumstances do change, there will be a chance that a set of genes, a species or a society will be able to continue under the new conditions. Diversity confers resilience, adaptability, and the capacity for regeneration.

5

Food Security, Food Quality, and Global Warming

The tools with which we have transformed farming practices—heavy machinery, mono-cultures, hybrid crop strains and chemicals—have caused enormous and often irreversible damage to soil fertility, water quality, public health, and viable farm economies. Moreover, the productivity of our farmland has become, year by year, ever more dependent on massive infusions of energy, both to produce and operate farm machinery and in the form of petrochemical-based fertilizers and pesticides.

Current estimates are that we expend more than three calories of energy to produce every calorie of food we eat. When the energy associated with all aspects of modern food systems—processing, packaging, transportation, and marketing—are included, the ratio becomes even more lopsided, with roughly 10 calories of energy in for every calorie of food energy out.

In this process of industrializing agricultural production, we have actually tied the future of farmland, which should be a renewable resource, to a non-renewable resource, fossil fuels. Unfortunately, the environmental consequences of this transformation of our food systems are largely unrecognized, as is the fact that at the root of these problems are the very economic and trade policies we are now entrenching in the WTO.

The free trade vision is of an integrated global agricultural economy, in which all regions of the world engage in the production of specialized agricultural commodities, and supply their needs in the global marketplace. Food is grown, not by farmers for local consumers, but by large corporations for global markets. The consequences of this global model for farmers in poor countries, who lose their subsistence farms to export producers, are of course disastrous *(see "Food Security" below)*, but for the moment consider the effects of this model on the energy intensity of agricultural production.

Agriculture, Trade, and Global Warming

As already noted, the globalization of food production and trade necessarily requires large-scale processing, packaging, and transportation systems, which in turn require enormous inputs of energy that will substantially increase consumption and use of fossil fuels. When account is taken of all of the energy inputs that support global food systems (for example, nearly 50% of all consumer packaging is used for food products), agriculture is probably the world's biggest business; in North America it historically used more energy and consumed more fossil fuel than any other industrial sector. By encouraging global food production, current trade policies will increase the energy demands of agricultural production and trade.

While governments have come to recognize the imperatives of averting global warming, and have undertaken to stabilize greenhouse-gas emissions at levels substantially lower than current levels in many developed countries, they have also embraced agricultural trade policies that will make it far more difficult, if not impossible, to achieve those goals. That environmental and agricultural trade policies could be at such cross-purposes is a testament to our failure to integrate environmental and economic policy.

Yet the Climate Change Convention exhorts governments to: "take precautionary measures to anticipate, prevent or minimize the causes of climate change and mitigate its adverse effects" [Art. 3, Principle 3], and to take "climate change considerations into account, to the extent feasible, in their relevant social, economic and environmental policies and actions... [Art 4 (f)]—all in an effort to "return by the end of the present decade to earlier levels of anthropogenic emissions of carbon dioxide and other greenhouse gases...." [Art.4 2(a)]

If governments are going to live up to the commitments they have made to combat climate change, they will have to examine seriously the energy consequences of resource, industrial, and agricultural policies. Moreover, if agricultural policies are to support less energy-intensive production, they will have to promote self-reliance in food production, not global dependence.

Food Security

"These deals aren't about free trade. They're about the right of these guys [U.S. multinationals] to do business the way they want, wherever they want..."
— *Eugene Whelan*
  Former Canadian Agriculture Minister

Another compelling reason to encourage self-reliant agricultural production is the severe risk of dependence on global production. To a great degree, this has become the plight of much of the Third World.

For several decades now, the character of global agricultural production had been driven by EU and U.S. farm policies. These in turn have been driven by the large agribusiness corporations that have benefited most from those policies, which have sought to secure the largest share of global markets for U.S. and European producers. To achieve this goal, two primary strategies have been adopted. The first is to keep international markets flooded with cheap agricultural commodities, which are often priced well below the cost of production. This has required massive farm subsidy programs in the U.S., the EU, as well as in other countries competing with them for export markets. The result of this competition has been enormous surpluses which are then dumped onto international markets.

While many poor countries have occasionally benefited from this abundance, in the bargain they have had to abandon any hope of establishing their own indigenous agricultural economies, leaving many entirely dependent on a continuing flow of subsidized grains and other food from the world's few exporters. In this vulnerable condition, supply disruptions, unstable currency rates, and wild swings in agricultural commodity prices have often meant widespread hunger and starvation.

The other strategy that the U.S. has used to achieve market dominance for its domestic producers has been to attack efforts by countries seeking self-reliance in agricultural production that may close their markets to U.S. exports. A primary target of these attacks has been supply management systems, such as those in place in Canada *(see "Supply Management" below)*.

In large measure these strategies have succeeded in garnering for U.S.-based agri-corporations the position of dominant players in global food markets. For example, in 1994 U.S. exports accounted for 36% of the wheat traded globally, 64% of the corn, barley, sorghum, and oats, 40% of the soybeans, 17% of the rice, and 33% of the cotton.[31] In many cases, only a few U.S. corporations account for this global market dominance. For example, 50% of U.S. grain exports in 1994 were accounted for by just two corporations.

The other important factor that has undermined food security for much of this planet's population has been very low commodity prices for Third World exports. Thus, as real prices for many commodities fell during the 1980s, pressures grew to increase production, particularly for developing countries dependent on agricultural exports to earn foreign exchange.

Caught in this squeeze between declining commodity prices and increasing debt loads, poor countries have been forced to engage in a cycle of desperation production. As prices fall, more and more land is appropriated for export production, production for local markets is displaced, and the ranks of landless peasants, no longer able to feed their families, continue to swell.

In response to this crisis, developed countries and large agri-corporations have cast the problem in terms of a shortage of food supplies, and have offered to fill the breach with more intensive production, biotechnology, pesticides, and fertilizers. Ignoring, as always, the fundamental question of wealth and resource distribution, free trade is again offered as the magic solution that will bring the prosperity people need to buy food in the global market. But there is no evidence to support a positive relationship between trade growth and food security. Indeed, as we have seen, the root causes of global food insecurity can in large part be found in the unregulated international marketplace, which has allowed wholesale export dumping by countries able to underwrite surplus food production in order to maintain global market shares. In fact, it is this very dynamic that has played a key role in creating downward pressure on commodity prices for Third World exports.

Describing how export agriculture can worsen the position of poor farmers, a document prepared by the FAO put it this way:

Because small-scale producers often lack the resources necessary to grow export-oriented crops, they may not be able to participate in this growth. On the contrary, they may find that commercial expansion has an inflationary effect on production costs and on land rent that may even make their traditional production less feasible. Small producers may abandon their land or be bought out by larger commercial interests.[32]

In fact, according to a recent OECD/World Bank study, much of the Third World will be net losers under new WTO rules, with the GDP of African countries actually dropping by 0.2-to-0.5%. Conversely, two-thirds of the expected increase in "global income" attributable to GATT will accrue to OECD countries that represent about one-third of our planet's human population.[33]

There are ways, however, in which agricultural policies can promote food security, and the most important of these would simply be to make food security the primary goal of agricultural production. Food policies, both international and national, would then encourage food production for local consumption first, and only secondarily for international markets. International trade and the activities of transnational corporations would also have to be closely regulated to ensure that they served, rather than undermined, the goal of a secure food supply.

Finally, food security would be defined as a basic human right—an objective opposed by the U.S. alone at the recent World Food Summit organized by the United Nations Food and Agriculture Organization (the FAO).[34]

Food Safety

Food safety and pesticide standards are subject to the provisions of the WTO Agreement on Sanitary and Phytosanitary Standards [SPS]. Again, trade jargon obscures the fact that this agreement primarily deals with food safety, biotechnology, pesticides, and other regulations concerning plants and animals. In many ways the SPS Agreement mirrors the provisions of the other WTO on standards: the Agreement on Technical Barriers to Trade (TBT), which is discussed in some detail in Chapter VIII (Environmental Standards). But the SPS Agreement actually goes further in constraining the scope for federal or provincial regulation.

To begin with, the SPS places a great emphasis on the need to harmonize food safety and pesticide regulations internationally, and includes several provisions compelling governments to adopt such standards on the one hand, while dramatically circumscribing the scope for national or local initiatives on the other. While the development of an international consensus around environmental standards may be a desirable objective, the effect of SPS harmonization rules is to create a ceiling, but no floor, for such regulations *(see discussion of the TBT).*

Another unique feature of the SPS regime that is very problematic can be found in several Articles that explicitly seek to reduce food safety and pesticide standards to scientific propositions to be determined by international science panels. A consensus of international scientific opinion then becomes the necessary precondition for environmental regulation. The absence of such a consensus can then be asserted as *prima facie* proof that trade protection motives must underlie a purported concern for the environment or food safety.

But the risks associated with pesticide residues in food or genetically modified organisms raise questions which go well beyond the competence of scientists to answer, because they involve complex ethical, social, and economic considerations. Therefore, not only are such rules fundamentally at odds with the precautionary principle, but they attempt to exclude from consideration a host of issues that require broad input and debate. Furthermore, by assigning the task of standard-setting to international technical bodies such as the Codex Alimentarius, the prerogatives of elected and accountable institutions are greatly diminished.

The first trade case to consider these new WTO rules concerned a challenge to a European ban on the importation of beef produced with the use of artificial growth hormones. The following case study illustrates the problems for food safety regulation created by this WTO Agreement.

Beef, Hormones, and the SPS

In early 1998, the WTO Appellate Body (AB) upheld a landmark trade decision which had found that the European Community (EC) was not entitled to maintain a ban on hormone-treated beef because it had failed to meet the requirements of the WTO, including the Agreement on Sanitary and Phytosanitary Standards (SPS). The trade complaints that had given rise to the ruling had been brought by Canada and the U.S., and were the first to invoke WTO rules as a weapon to challenge food safety and health protection measures. True to form, whenever trade rules have collided with other policy objectives, the AB has had little difficulty in concluding that European concerns about public health would have to give way to trade objectives.

In what has become a consistent pattern of trade dispute resolution under WTO rules, the trade dispute panel that was convened to hear the complaint came down hard in favour of trade liberalization goals—in this case even holding that the burden of proof in the case lay with the EU. On appeal, however, the AB was more circumspect and measured in its critique, but not to the point of actually upholding the health protection measure at issue.

The EC ban on the importation of beef treated with hormones had been established in response to widespread consumer concern about the health risks associated with hormone residues in meat—risks that were difficult to quantify. Canada and the U.S. argued that the ban was not consistent with the standard-setting requirements of either the TBT, SPS, or GATT 1994 Agreements of the WTO. Both a dispute panel (in a 472-page decision) and the AB agreed.

Among the most troubling aspects of the AB decision is its rejection of the precautionary principle as a justifiable basis upon which health protection measures might be established. The precautionary principle is a cornerstone of domestic and international environmental law that recognizes the importance of regulatory action to avoid certain risks, even in advance of being able to prove them. The principle is enshrined in several international environmental agreements, and has even been accepted by the International Chamber of Commerce. For example, the Convention on Biological Diversity adopts the principle by recognizing that it is vital to anticipate and prevent environmental harm. Where significant threat of harm exists, lack of full scientific certainty should not be used as a reason for postponing measures to avoid or minimize the harm.

PCBs, cigarette smoking, leaded gasoline, thalidomide, and asbestos are a few among many examples of the wisdom of being safe rather than sorry. But, according to the AB, the precautionary principle must give way to the explicit wording of the SPS when conflicts arise. The decision should sound alarm bells for both consumers and governments persuaded of the need for food safety measures, even in the absence of demonstrable proof or an international scientific consensus that action is warranted.

Almost as problematic was the AB's ruling that, under the SPS, decisions about food safety will also now have to be based on formal risk assessment processes. But, while risk assessment is offered by the AB as a reliable and scientific basis for regulation, many observers doubt the validity of this approach—on both scientific and ethical grounds—for estimating the consequences of exposure to substances about which very little is known.

The ruling also greatly elevates the importance of the standards established by the Codex Alimentarius Commission, an international standard-setting body. According to the WTO Appellate Body, Codex standards will now operate as an effective ceiling for all food safety or health protection measures. Yet Codex, which is based and operates in Geneva, is an institution that is singularly inaccessible to all but a handful of international corporations and business associations that are capable of maintaining delegations in Geneva. Not surprisingly, Codex standards often fall substantially short of those established by jurisdictions closer and more responsive to the interests and views of consumers and health advocates. The beef hormone case now casts a long shadow over any standard that goes further than the international norms established by Codex.

The WTO Agreement on Agriculture

Until the advent of the WTO, agricultural trade had not been subject to most GATT disciplines, and several GATT rules specifically exempted agricultural measures, such as supply management and import controls. These exceptions reflected the interests of many countries that wished to keep their domestic policies free from GATT scrutiny. Among them were countries providing domestic producers with massive subsidies that inevitably resulted in overproduction and export dumping—practices that would have been clearly at odds with GATT rules.

For poorer countries, the imposition of export-driven agricultural policies was accomplished through other means. For example, structural adjustment programs imposed by international banking and lending institutions have often denied developing countries the opportunity to establish the self-reliant agricultural policies that GATT exceptions would have otherwise allowed.

However, as agricultural subsidies continued to escalate in the war to secure export markets, they began to represent a serious drain on public finances of food-exporting nations. Determined to extricate itself from this ascending spiral, the U.S. seized upon Uruguay Round negotiations as the venue to resolve the subsidies imbroglio. In fact, agricultural trade reform became such an important issue that it threatened to scuttle the entire negotiations on more than one occasion. Thus the WTO final agreement was only reached when the U.S. and the European Union were able to hammer out a deal to gradually reduce farm subsidies over time.

As part of the arrangement to submit agricultural policies to the full constraint of trade disciplines, and much to the disadvantage of poorer nations, the agreement on agriculture also called for the removal of exemptions for import controls and supply management regimes. As part of this compromise, developed countries agreed to reduce subsidies to their agricultural producers. At first the reduction of such subsidies would appear to benefit poorer countries wishing to establish their own farm economies or compete for export markets. But, as several developing country NGOs have pointed out,[35] the reduction of Northern price supports would actually mean very little, because under the WTO agreement on agriculture:

- Rich countries will still provide direct subsidies to producers for many years to come. Current commitments only foresee a 36% reduction in subsidies over the next six years, and some tariffs may be reduced by as little as 15%. There is no limit on the use of indirect subsidies to farmers as long as these are not linked to actual production.

- Without the resources to subsidize farmers, the only way poor countries could support local agricultural production was to use import quotas. WTO rules now prohibit import controls.

- While poor countries can replace import controls and quotas with tariffs, unstable monetary values and sudden currency fluctuations can easily make those tariffs meaningless.

- Finally, tariffs represent a much less precise or reliable way to balance local production with imports, and that balance can be easily disturbed by macroeconomic factors that poor countries can rarely foresee, let alone influence.

For these reasons, the commitment to reduce farm subsidies is unlikely to have any meaningful impact on the enormous market distortions that current practices have created. Furthermore, developing countries have lost the few tools they had to support domestic producers. Finally, given the overall impacts of the new WTO regime, which includes seed-patent protection and the removal of foreign investment controls, it is likely that the brave new world of agricultural trade reform will, for poor countries, simply mean another large dose of the "medicine" that ails them.

Supply Management

When environmental concern about agricultural production has arisen, it has largely been focused on the impacts of pesticide and fertilizer use. Similarly, consumer concerns have concentrated on food safety. Unfortunately, little attention has been paid to the economic and structural underpinnings of agricultural policy which have given rise to the environmental and food safety issues that are symptomatic of those policies and practices.

The impacts of trade rules on agricultural production oblige us to examine the underlying economic and trade policies that have given rise to, and now seek to entrench, the unsustainable agricultural practices that are laying waste to farmland, adulterating food quality, causing ground and surface water pollution on a massive scale, and substantially accelerating our use of fossil fuels.

If we are to establish sustainable forms of agricultural production, we must find ways to reshape economic and trade policies so they will support rather than undermine these efforts. An important place to begin is with the realization that there is no sustainable agricultural production without farmers. While restoring a stable and viable rural agricultural economy is obviously not a sufficient condition for sustainable agricultural production, it is definitely a necessary one. To assess the impact of WTO rules on rural farm economies, we have to consider what those rules will do to supply-management systems in Canada.

Stable prices and predictable demand are essential to the viability of relatively small-scale agricultural producers. But price instability is an inherent feature of all commodity markets. Thus, unpredictable commodity prices and market speculation have overwhelmed the capacity of millions of farmers to withstand the shock of wildly fluctuating revenues and steadily increasing costs. To aggravate these pressures, farmers must also negotiate commodity prices with large food-processing and distribution companies that represent their primary markets. Their relative bargaining power in this relationship is negligible.

In this way, many of the dynamics that have wreaked such havoc on Third World agricultural economies have also had severe impacts on the rural farm economies of developed countries. The result has been hundreds of thousands of farm bankruptcies, highly exploitative and unsustainable farm practices, and the wholesale use of public funds to underwrite the profits of large agri-corporations. In Canada, however, we have been able to significantly moderate the impact of global market forces by adopting and guarding a successful supply-management system for several agricultural commodities. In fact Canada's supply-management systems have been the model that farmers in other countries have urged their own governments to adopt.

As explained by Lise-Anne Delorme, an Ottawa Valley dairy farmer, "The supply–management system is the very foundation of rural Canada. Abandon the system that makes farms like ours viable, and the underpinnings of the entire rural economy are destroyed."

Under supply management, farmers must sell to marketing boards which negotiate a collective price for those products with domestic and foreign buyers. In order to create stable prices, marketing boards also regulate supply to avoid overproduction. Hence the appellation: supply management. The viability of domestic supply management in turn depends upon being able to control imports so as not to disrupt the domestic balance of supply and demand, and there is the rub. As we have seen, imposing quantitative import restrictions is at odds with GATT Article XI, which prohibits such import controls.

Until the establishment of the WTO, the special circumstances of agricultural production meant that supply management was recognized as a valid exception to GATT rules. However, for many years the U.S. has been an outspoken critic of supply management, and on numerous occasions U.S. politicians and agencies have declared their intention to see these Canadian programs dismantled. Indeed, several trade challenges have been made to that end. It is not surprising then that, as the driving force behind the new agricultural trade agreement, the U.S. was able to insist that protection for supply management programs be removed from WTO rules. The loss is clearly a devastating blow to supply management in Canada.

However, because high tariffs can still be substituted for import controls, Canada has been able to maintain its supply-management systems, notwithstanding the removal of this exemption. By using tariffs to regulate the inflow of agricultural commodities, Canada can take some steps to protect supply-management systems and preserve an ongoing role for the marketing boards that oversee the system. But, without an explicit exception in WTO rules, supply management is certainly much more vulnerable to trade challenge. Moreover, tariffs will have to be reduced over time, and campaigns by free trade proponents, both within and outside Canada, continue to pressure governments to abandon these programs.

Intellectual Property Rights

One other important aspect of the WTO agenda affecting agriculture should be noted here. This is the WTO Agreement on Trade-Related Intellectual Property Rights, which is discussed later under its own heading.

A Citizen's Agenda

We have over the years displaced farmers and farm labour with pesticides, energy-based fertilizers, heavy machinery, and biotechnology. We have done so at a horrendous cost to the environment, food security, and the viability of rural communities. If an ecological recovery of agricultural lands is to be brought about, three basic objectives must be accomplished. First, the economic viability of farm communities must be revitalized. The family farm is still one of the best models for the notion of one generation holding resources in trust for the next.

Secondly, agricultural policies and practices must seek to reduce the energy required by every aspect of our food systems. And, thirdly, the overall policy goal of sustainable farm production must be food security—not more trade.

If present trends are to be reversed, consumers and environmentalists will have to build alliances with farmers and farm organizations to confront the agenda of global agri-corporations. They can begin by advocating those policies that will begin to restore agricultural production and trade to a sustainable footing by:

- reducing the distance between farm and consumer (between garden and table) which in turn would reduce the need for food processing and packaging, and transportation;

- recycling organic wastes, adopting integrative pest-control programs, and otherwise substituting organic for chemical inputs;

- applying ecologically derived cropping patterns and other management techniques to conserve soil;

- banning the use of genetically modified organisms for food production;

- using renewable sources of energy;

- creating stable agricultural economies to keep farmers on the land; and by

- embracing food security as the primary goal of agricultural production.

In other words, by making the transition from global dependence to self-reliance.

6

Forests, Fish, and Water

Concerns about the environmental implications of international trade have focused almost exclusively on environmental standards. Relatively little has been done to reveal or address the impacts of global trade rules on our options for achieving sustainable resource management goals, or for preserving biodiversity. In fact, issues that link trade and natural resources are not even on the agenda of the WTO Committee on Trade and Environment. Yet, over the longer term, the impact of free trade on natural resources and biodiversity will likely be its most destructive legacy.

There are two basic observations that can be made about the character of international trade in natural resources. The first is that most of the world's natural resources (roughly 80%) are consumed by the 20% of us who live in developed countries. The second is that developing countries have effectively been denied the economic development that comes from processing raw resources and converting them into manufactured goods.

Two aspects of trade law and practice establish and reinforce these inequitable and historic trade patterns. First, Article XI of the GATT, as we have seen, prohibits export controls, whether to support domestic manufacturing or for any other purpose. Second, the practice of tariff escalation, adopted by developed countries, imposes higher tariffs on manufactured goods than on the raw materials used to produce them.

Export controls are an important part of a larger strategy to conserve resources and foster local economic development. WTO rules, however, prohibit such controls for these purposes. Tariff escalation, which discriminates against value-added products, similarly undermines sustainable resource management.

Export Control as a Resource-Conservation Tool

Over the years, many governments have imposed raw-resource export bans in order to conserve those resources and to promote local economic development. (Canadian examples include bans on the export of raw logs and unprocessed fish.) Such export controls can have an immediate and obvious impact on the rate of resource exploitation; most often, however, such controls are used to ensure that value was added (processing or manufacturing) to raw resources before export.

For resource-based communities, export controls created a more dynamic and diverse economy, and ultimately a greater stake in ensuring sustainable resource management. For government, the result was greater tax revenue from the additional economic activity taking place within its jurisdiction. This, in turn, created the fiscal resources needed for governments to invest in resource enhancement and conservation measures—and provided a stronger rationale for doing so, as such public expenditures would now benefit processing and manufacturing, as well as the harvesting or extraction industries.

From an environmental perspective, there is one other important reason to support the processing of resources close to the source of their primary production or extraction: the enormous energy and other environmental costs of transporting unprocessed resources over great distances. As we have seen, the transportation impacts of global production and trade represent a very substantial and largely uncounted cost of the global economy.[36]

Conversely, without the ability to ban the export of unprocessed natural resources, resource-based economies become poorer and less diverse. Income, both to the private and public sectors, becomes dependent on the rate at which the resource is extracted, and local economies become far more vulnerable to commodity-price swings. When commodity prices decline, enormous pressure is exerted to increase the rate of resource exploitation, to eliminate regulatory controls, and/or to reduce royalties, as we have seen on many occasions and in many communities across Canada. These dynamics can currently be observed in the forest-resource sector of British Columbia, where, in response to market pressures, industry is lobbying government to abandon forest-harvesting regulations, reduce stumpage fees, and even privatize Crown forest land.

Export Controls and Article XI

For these reasons, the ability to control resource exports is crucial to the development of sustainable resource management programs. Yet it is precisely this prerogative that free trade agreements seek to remove. Admittedly, export bans provide no guarantee that governments will implement sustainable resource management strategies. Indeed resource-export controls have done little to avert serious problems now common in virtually all resource sectors. However, without the authority to regulate exports, governments simply won't have the capability to shift policy in a more sustainable direction, no matter how compelling the environmental or economic imperatives for doing so.

In other words, just when the need to fundamentally overhaul current resource management policies has become undeniably clear, free trade seeks to remove the mechanisms needed to change our present and unsustainable course.

Export Controls and Tariff Escalation

As noted, tariff escalation imposes higher import tariffs on manufactured goods than on the raw materials from which they are made. Thus, a bale of raw cotton receives more favourable tariff treatment than does the same bale woven into textiles, and more favourable still than garments made from those textiles. Although GATT Article XI precludes quantitative import restrictions, it does allow countries to use duties, tariffs, and other charges to regulate international trade. Thus, tariff escalation policies can be adopted to effectively accomplish the quantitative trade controls that Article XI would otherwise preclude.

The effect of tariff escalation policies has been to ensure that the value-added processing of resources harvested, extracted, or mined in poor countries is carried out in richer industrial countries. This in large measure explains why the economies of most developing countries remain closely tied to primary commodities, which account for most of their export earnings: Latin America (67%), West Asia (84%), and Sub-Saharan Africa (92%). To exacerbate this dependence, the real price of commodities has been declining since 1980, intensifying pressure to exploit natural resources as countries struggle to maintain export earnings.

The ability of developed countries to maintain high tariffs is lessening; and, under the WTO, some progress has been made in reducing the scope for tariff escalation. However, as competition for scarce resources increases, securing access to dwindling supplies remains a high priority for the North. Therefore, other means are being devised to secure access to the energy and raw materials needed to support Northern processing and manufacturing industries.

Thus as developed countries have to abandon their policies of tariff escalation, they are now making increasing use of Article XI to assure the continued flow of raw materials to their manufacturing industries. The U.S., for example, has used this provision to challenge efforts by Argentina to control the export of unprocessed hides (to support its domestic tanning and leather goods industry) and to undermine Canadian raw log- and fish-export controls (discussed below).

Undeniably, such practices have fundamentally undercut the economic aspirations of developing countries. If sustainable development means a more equitable distribution of the world's resources, and of the economic benefits derived therefrom, then current trade rules will need to be changed to encourage the domestic processing and manufacturing of indigenous resources. As they stand, they simply perpetuate the patterns of development that have impoverished much of the world and laid waste its resources.

Forests

Across Canada, environmentalists have struggled to protect our forests from unsustainable forestry policies and practices. Despite wide variations in forest ecosystems and operations, common concerns include unsustainable levels of logging; ecologically damaging forestry practices; lack of biodiversity protection; poor levels and quality of regeneration; and unsettled First Nations' land claims.

Environmentalists are well aware that policies addressing the use and conservation of natural resources are fundamental to both environmental protection and the integration of environmental and economic goals. However, as we have seen, trade rules dramatically curtail the policy and regulatory options that are needed to support conservation. Moreover, the few remaining options may fall victim to the internecine warfare of U.S. and Canadian lumber interests.

Canadian forest-management practices have repeatedly come under fire from the U.S. lumber lobby, which for years has had to compete with cheap Canadian lumber exports. Several trade disputes have been initiated on behalf of U.S. producers, challenging Canadian policies and low stumpage rates. To U.S. interests, these represent unfair subsidies to Canadian mills.

With some reservations, environmentalists on both sides of the border have welcomed this attention, as these trade disputes have brought to light the "fire sale" prices at which public forests have been assigned to large forest-industry corporations. However, one important aspect of these disputes—the issue of raw log-export controls—has been largely overlooked. Accordingly, the following summary describes how these Canadian export controls got caught in the crossfire of the Canada-U.S. lumber wars.

This case also illustrates how trade disputes can be used tactically to keep governments from adopting resource-export controls even when specific exemptions from trade agreements would ostensibly allow their use. While the dispute proceeded under the provisions of NAFTA, the principles of trade policy articulated by the panel would be equally applicable to the WTO.

The Case of Canadian Raw Log-Export Controls

Because log-export controls are of special importance to the economies of several states and provinces, NAFTA explicitly exempts them from the rules of free trade that apply to natural resources. (in Annex 301.3). Nevertheless, the U.S. Commerce Department (DOC) spurred on by the U.S. lumber lobby, initiated a challenge to Canadian log-export controls under the U.S. Tariff Act.

Because NAFTA prevented the DOC from going after these export controls directly, it challenged Canadian log-export bans as conferring a subsidy on the Canadian lumber industry. Subsidies are generally prohibited as unfair trade practices by the rules of free trade. When subsidies are given despite this prohibition, trade rules authorize the use of countervailing import duties to "level the playing field" for domestic producers.

In this case, the DOC argued that log-export restrictions artificially inflate domestic supply, which in turn lowers prices to local mills. Thus, the DOC asserted, Canada's export controls had conferred an "indirect subsidy" on its lumber industries, which could be countervailed.

The dispute panel ultimately rejected the validity of the DOC claim on technical grounds, but it did support the claim that export controls could be treated as unfair subsidies. In doing so, the panel's decision represented a dramatic departure from past practice, effectively extending the reach of countervail rules to a broad range of resource policies.

The same tactics might be used by the U.S., or another developed country, to attack a high export tariff on unprocessed resources, even if the tariff was otherwise consistent with WTO rules. More importantly, by allowing countervail relief every time some action by government reduces the cost of production for domestic producers, a host of environmental and other programs become vulnerable to challenge. Indeed, as argued in a dissent to this ruling, an emission trading program that allows polluters greater flexibility in meeting environmental goals at lower costs could be considered a countervailable subsidy. Indeed, taken to its logical conclusion, such reasoning must see all conservation measures as distorting supply and demand, and therefore vulnerable to attack as unfair trading practices.

The case also suggests that exclusions such as that in NAFTA for raw log-export controls may not be worth the paper they are written on if they run counter to the prevailing orthodoxy of trade deregulation. For, even though raw log-export controls are specifically identified as an allowable exception to NAFTA prohibitions on export controls, and endorsed as such by the NAFTA partners, the softwood trade panel had little difficulty endorsing an argument that virtually rendered this exception meaningless.

The broad implications of this ruling are disturbing. Consider, for example, what this decision means should Canada refuse inter-basin water transfers to the U.S. The argument would be made that, by prohibiting the export of water, Canada had conferred a countervailable subsidy on Canadian farmers and industry—the value of the subsidy being the difference in cost between Canadian and free market prices. Moreover, the extravagant and unsustainable U.S. water use and pricing policies that might have given rise to these price differentials would be entirely irrelevant under present trade dispute rules.

Forest-Practices Certification as Eco-labelling

To take advantage of the internationalization of standard-setting, and to promote trade in forest products, the Canadian Pulp and Paper Association and the Canadian Standards Association (CSA) have developed a voluntary certification system for sustainable forest management (SFM). Essentially an eco-labelling scheme, its stated purpose is to enable purchasers to identify products from sustainably managed forests controlled by companies whose practices are assessed by independent certifiers.

Environmentalists roundly criticized this scheme, for several reasons. First, it would certify management systems without requiring environmental protection performance standards. Secondly, it would not require a chain of custody that would ensure that products actually come from certified forests. Finally, it was developed in a flawed, industry-dominated process.

In 1995, the CSA attempted to have its proposal adopted for international standard-setting by the International Standards Organization (ISO), but international environmental opposition prompted its withdrawal.

The Forest Stewardship Council

The Forest Stewardship Council (FSC) is an international organization composed of environmentalists, social justice groups, industry, and indigenous peoples. It has also established a voluntary certification scheme for forest products, but based on principles and forest standards that environmentalists consider credible. Newly established in Canada, the FSC will require that Canadian standards be developed on a regional basis, given the different forest types in Canada. The FSC "certifies the certifiers," but unlike the CSA process set out above, it includes principles for performance, and a chain-of-custody requirement to identify products from a given managed forest.

Although still a small organization, it has become an important player in the international forest trade, and a potentially potent ally in the marketing of environmentally preferred forest products.

The federal and provincial governments of Canada have supported the industry-dominated CSA certification scheme. At the WTO Committee on Trade and Environment, Canada has argued that voluntary non-governmental eco-labelling schemes such as the Forest Stewardship Council should be subject to GATT disciplines. (Because trade rules prohibit measures that discriminate against "like" products on the basis of how they are produced, the FSC model would clearly contravene WTO rules.)

Fisheries

Fisheries-related trade disputes provide further evidence of the clash between trade rules and conservation objectives. The Tuna-Dolphin rulings (discussed above) illustrate the ways in which GATT rules create substantial obstacles to environmental initiatives that seek to protect global or extraterritorial resources. A recent case arising under the WTO provided a test of the new regime's tolerance of conservation programs directed at global marine resources. The ruling, while couched in somewhat different terms, was just as dismissive of these goals as the Tuna- Dolphin decisions had been.

Shrimp-Turtles[37]—Tuna-Dolphins revisited

In January 1997, India and a number of countries from Southeast Asia invoked the dispute-resolution procedures of the WTO to challenge a ban imposed by the United States on the importation of shrimp and shrimp products. In a case with many similarities to the Tuna-Dolphin cases, the heart of this dispute again involved U.S. marine-mammal protection legislation.

The environmental regulation at issue was the requirement that commercial shrimp trawlers operating in sea-turtle habitat employ "turtle excluder devices," which would permit sea turtles to escape from shrimp nets before drowning. The U.S. argued that it was levelling the playing field for domestic shrimpers, who were subject to the same regulations. Again, Third World countries complained about the imperialistic character of U.S. law, and argued it was implemented in a way that unfairly discriminated against foreign producers.

In April 1998, a WTO dispute-settlement panel wasted little time in concluding that the U.S. import ban was "clearly a threat to the multilateral trading system," and Article XX of the GATT did not apply. In fact, the panel appears to have been so offended by the U.S. legislation that it felt obliged to charge that it represented a "threat" or "put at risk" or "undermined" the world trading system on no less than nine occasions.

However, as has now become the norm in such cases, and in a manner that further undermines any expectation of consistent reasoning in trade cases involving environmental measures, a subsequent review of the panel's ruling by the WTO Appelate Body (AB) rejected its reasoning, but not its conclusion. In an apparent effort to calm some of the waters stirred up by the panel's intemperate language, the AB used more measured and even conciliatory language. It also took the unprecedented step of receiving three briefs submitted by NGOs, included as part of the submissions to the panel by the U.S. government.

However, the AB found no less than seven distinct grounds upon which to find the U.S. import ban to be in violation of WTO rules. As in all other trade cases involving environmental initiatives, the AB had no hesitation in substituting its judgment for that of legislators and public officials. Nor was the AB apparently troubled by the sweeping implications of its conclusion that, in order to satisfy WTO requirements, the U.S. would have to afford foreign producers the same standing and rights of judicial appeal against regulatory initiatives as are available to its own citizens. In other words, to guard against potential future trade challenges, governments must effectively invite any foreign producer that might in some way be affected by its initiative to take it to court.

The notion that a national government must grant foreign parties the right to invoke domestic administrative and judicial remedies, should they feel aggrieved by some environmental or conservation initiative, would be dismissed as preposterous in any other context. But, according to the logic of globalization, the AB had no apparent qualms in offering such a requirement as the necessary test of WTO compatibility.

Finally, notwithstanding the complex and often convoluted reasoning of these trade decisions, it is important not to lose sight of the fact that at issue in these disputes are environmental measures established, not for purpose of interfering with trade, but in good faith, to achieve important conservation and biodiversity objectives. Of course, some domestic businesses will invariably benefit from increased measures of environmental protection and resource conservation. In fact, rewarding companies that harvest sustainably, recycle wastes, and reduce energy use is an important goal of many environmental laws. But, under WTO rules, the very existence of such corporate winners now becomes the basis for impugning such standards as tainted by domestic economic benefits.

Export Controls as a Domestic Fisheries Management Tool

Closer to home, but equally revealing of the impact of free trade on fisheries conservation measures, are two trade cases concerning salmon and herring fisheries off Canada's west coast. Both involved U.S. challenges to Canadian fisheries regulations. The first of these disputes proceeded under GATT, the second under the Canada–U.S. Free Trade Agreement.[38] However, the GATT rules central to both cases apply equally to NAFTA and the WTO.

These cases also illustrate how the two trade regimes often work together, to deliver a one-two punch to resource conservation policies. As the Tuna-Dolphin decisions illustrate, WTO trade rules create impediments to international marine conservation. The salmon and herring cases show how the same rules work to undermine efforts to manage domestic fisheries and marine ecosystems.

In order to establish sustainable management regimes for coastal fisheries, governments must be able to impose effective controls upon all those exploiting marine resources within these zones. For the domestic fishing industry serving local markets, the exercise is reasonably straightforward, and governments have created regulatory mechanisms to control what, when, where, and how much is taken from coastal zones. While these regulatory regimes have failed dismally in many instances, sufficient authority did exist to establish sustainable management programs, had it been properly exercised.

However, as the following trade disputes illustrate, free trade has now virtually eliminated this authority at the very time it is most needed.

The Salmon and Herring Cases

In 1908, Canada passed a regulation under the Canadian Fisheries Act prohibiting the export of unprocessed salmon and herring. Because the salmon and herring fisheries represented a large share of Canada's west coast fishery, the export embargo created a thriving processing and canning industry, which has been an important part of the economy of British Columbia for most of this century. In 1986, however, the U.S. used GATT rules to challenge Canada's Fisheries Act regulations as part of its efforts to secure a larger share of the fishery for its own canning industry. The challenge appears to have been the first taken under GATT rules concerning an export-control measure.

In defence of its program, Canada argued that its export limits represented an integral element of its long-standing fishery management regime, which included habitat protection, catch limits, international agreements, and monitoring and enforcement systems. The overall effect of this comprehensive regime was conservation. However, Canada also readily conceded that its export prohibition was multi-purposed and intended to also ensure the viability of Canada's fish-processing industry. This objective, it argued, was entirely consistent with conservation goals, because it allowed Canada to justify significant public expenditures on salmon-enhancement programs in the expectation that benefits would flow to all sectors of the fishing industry, not just to the harvesters.

Unpersuaded by these arguments, the GATT panel found Canada's export controls to be contrary to GATT rules and to be indefensible under the "resource conservation" exception (Art. XX(g)) of GATT's general prohibition against export controls

(Art. XI). In response, Canada revoked the regulation that had been a cornerstone of its fishery management regime for 80 years, and substituted one that required that all salmon and herring be landed in Canada for inspection and biological sampling before being exported.

Canada insisted that this measure was necessary to ensure that fishing limits were respected. It also argued that biological sampling was critical to the success of species conservation and management goals. However, landing requirements also meant that this Canadian catch would be processed in Canadian canning factories. The U.S. filed another trade complaint.

The ensuing dispute was the first decided under the Canada–U.S. Free Trade Agreement (FTA), and was decided in favour of the U.S. Undeterred by the fact that Canadian regulations set no restrictions on the export of fish to the U.S., the panel found Canadian landing requirements to be in breach of the prohibition on export controls set out in GATT Article XI. (As noted, GATT rules are incorporated as a base line for the FTA and NAFTA.)

The panel then considered whether Canadian regulations might be justified as an exception under GATT Article XX(g), as a measure "relating to the conservation of exhaustible natural resources if such measures are made effective in conjunction with restrictions on domestic production or consumption." It reasoned that, to qualify as an exception under this rule, an export embargo would have to be "primarily aimed at conservation."

Apart from the absence of any support for such a test in the text of the FTA, one might regard this precondition as a reasonable standard. However, in the panel's view, "primarily" meant that such a measure "would have been adopted for conservation reasons alone," and that the purpose could not have been accomplished by other means. This is a test that few, if any, environmental regulations could pass, particularly when administered by trade bureaucrats.

As was true of the earlier GATT decision, the FTA panel refused to distinguish between the rights of domestic and foreign fish-processing industries. While this is entirely consistent with the rules of free trade, it is fundamentally incompatible with the principle that the opportunity to exploit a resource must bear some relationship to the responsibility to manage and care for it. By giving foreign resource companies the same access to coastal fish resources as that enjoyed by domestic producers, free trade has imported into the sphere of domestic resource management the problem that has plagued the global commons, i.e., opportunity for all to exploit and responsibility for none to conserve.

The salmon and herring decisions run true to form in asserting the primacy of trade policy objectives and letting impacts on natural resources fall where they may. While GATT rules may look like the villain here, it is really the combined effect of the FTA (now NAFTA) and GATT (now the WTO) that close off every avenue of trade regulation of resource exports.

As noted, under the WTO countries are free to use pricing—i.e., export taxes or royalties—to control the export of resources. In other words, while GATT Article XI prohibits quantitative export controls, it allows a country to establish a two-price resource policy—one for domestic consumers and another for exporters. However, the FTA and NAFTA specifically close off this public-policy option. Neither of the salmon and herring cases would have arisen but for Canada's obligations under the FTA and NAFTA to remove differential taxation of its natural resources.

Before leaving the subject of export controls, it is also important to note that NAFTA goes much further than the WTO in virtually eliminating the authority of governments to restrict exports, even in times of critical shortage. Article 315 of NAFTA establishes a regime of proportional access that would allow the U.S processors, for example, perpetual access to west-coast fisheries resources in the same proportion that market forces allow them at any time to acquire. In other words, this right will persist no matter how severe the impacts of resource depletion may become.

Free Trade and Sustainable Resource Management

The trade cases summarized above expose some of the problems that arise when the principles of free trade are applied to the resources sector. If governments are to establish sustainable resource management policies, they must have full control over foreign investment in the resource sector. They must also be able to control exports, both for the purposes of conservation and to create value-added and more diverse resource economies. Under WTO rules, these prerogatives are fundamentally undermined.

For far too long, we have been exploiting our forests, fisheries, farmland, and other resources as if they were limitless. Critical shortages are now apparent in virtually every resource sector, including coastal fisheries, forests, water, and energy. Yet, now that the imperatives to change our course are clear, the WTO and the free trade agenda would entrench the very resource management practices that have created our present predicament.

As Canada has moved to deregulate many sectors of our domestic economy, environmental laws are coming under unprecedented attack at both the federal and provincial levels. Devolution of federal environmental powers to the provinces is reducing federal leadership in environmental law-making, and environmentalists working for new policies are dismissed with the claim that the trade agreements don't allow them. If rules of trade are to serve rather than to undermine the principles of sustainable development, they must be fundamentally overhauled to make a virtue, rather than a sin, of resource conservation.

Water

There is no resource that is more essential to biodiversity, social and economic development—and indeed, civilization itself—than water.[39] Growing scarcity and widespread misuse of water pose a serious and growing threat to sustainable development and all aspects of human health and welfare, food security, industrial development, and the ecosystems on which these all depend.

Worldwide, the consumption of water has increased over twice as much as the growth of the world's population in the last century. The United Nations has determined that, with current water use patterns, by 2025 over two-thirds of the world's population, or 5.5 billion people, will suffer from water shortage.[40]

For much of this planet's human population, potable water is already in critically short supply, and the lack of sufficient water resources to support food production is emerging as one of the most urgent crises of our time. The impact of climate change on water and hydrologic cycles, and the complex interrelationship between degraded and depleted water resources and biodiversity loss, underscore the vast global dimensions of the problems we confront.

To many Canadians, these problems may seem distant and of little relevance to a country so well-endowed with water resources. But, while it is true that Canadians still have an abundance of riches when it comes to water, any notion that we can ignore the global and international dimensions of the problems that affect this resource simply ignores the interrelatedness of global ecosystems and economies. Moreover, scientists have warned Canadians that pollution, habitat destruction and global warming will so compromise our own fresh-water supplies that fresh-water fisheries could disappear and drinking water supplies be put into a state of crisis. Unless we change course dramatically, they warn that fresh water will become Canada's foremost ecological crisis in this century.[41]

In other words, we are squandering Canada's enormously rich water resource endowment through indifference and neglect. Indeed, the consequences of our failure to act as responsible water stewards has already had very serious impacts in Canada—from the devastating effects of massive water diversion projects on regional ecosystems, to the impacts of waterborne disease outbreaks for local communities. The tragedy in Walkerton, Ontario, serves as a terrible reminder of just how immediate, human, and severe these impacts can be.

Water as a Tradeable Commodity

Recent proposals to export Canadian water, and an investor-state suit under NAFTA concerning B.C.'s water export control measures *(see insert)*, have revived Canadian concerns about the loss of public control over this vital resource. In response, the federal government has announced several initiatives, including the negotiation of a federal- provincial accord to ban bulk water exports, and strengthening the Boundary Waters Treaty Act.[42] Its strategy, however, appears to have been determined by a reluctance to confront the reality that, under NAFTA and WTO rules, water export controls are prohibited. Moreover, under NAFTA, and to a lesser extent the WTO, Canada is also precluded from denying foreign investors and service providers the same access to Canadian water it allows Canadian companies, communities, and residents.

But, instead of seeking amendments to these international trade agreements, Canada is attempting to finesse these trade constraints by taking the approach that water in its "natural state" is not a tradeable "good" and therefore not subject to international trade rules.

Notwithstanding its longstanding assurances that Canadian water would not be sacrificed to its trade ambitions, the federal government now acknowledges that its obligations under NAFTA and the WTO have substantially limited its options. In a paper prepared for the Canadian Council of Environment Ministers,[43] it has conceded that trade considerations led it to shift its approach from a federal ban on water exports to a focus on a federal–provincial accord to prohibit bulk removal of water from Canada's drainage basins. The essential premise of this initiative is that, by adopting a "watershed approach," Canada can avoid the strictures of its international trade obligations.

But no analysis or argument is offered to support this assertion, other than a statement ostensibly made by the three NAFTA Parties in 1993 (the 1993 Statement) providing:

> Unless water, in any form, has entered into commerce and becomes a good or product, it is not covered by the provisions of any trade agreement, including the NAFTA. And nothing in the NAFTA would oblige any NAFTA Party to either exploit its water for commercial use, or to begin exporting water in any form. Water in its natural state in lakes, rivers, reservoirs, aquifers, water basins and the like is not a good or product, is not traded, and therefore is not and never has been subject to the terms of any trade agreement.

Thus, to avoid running afoul of the prohibition against export controls, the federal government reasons that it must focus its efforts on regulating "water resources," which it argues would not be considered a "good" under GATT rules.

Unfortunately, there are several reasons to doubt the viability of this strategy. To begin with, water in its natural state is considered a commercial good under U.S. law. In fact, U.S. courts have consistently concluded that groundwater is an article of commerce, rejecting the argument that state governments have the authority to discriminate between in-state and out-of-state water use.[44] Summarizing U.S. law on this point, a recent report by a panel of U.S. and Canadian legal experts to the Governors of Great Lakes States concluded that "arguments that water is not a good are not persuasive" and "indeed... run contrary to the United States' own jurisprudence with respect to the characterization of water as an article of commerce..."[45]

Second, water is also considered a good under international law. The European Court of Justice has interpreted the term "good" to include anything capable of monetary valuation and of being the object of a commercial transaction. It has also held that the term "goods" includes not only the sale of goods, but goods and materials that are supplied as services. In other words, if water is being used to provide a service, such as providing water for public consumption or agricultural irrigation, then it is considered a good under the EC Treaty.[46]

But, even if one were to accept the dubious proposition that "entered into commerce" is the appropriate standard to determine the application of trade rules to water, a very substantial proportion of Canadian water resources would have to be viewed as already having "entered commerce." Consider, for instance, that a very large proportion of Canadian water resources are already subject to commercial use: to generate power, to produce manufactured commodities and goods, or to irrigate crops. Indeed, in many areas, water supplies have actually been overcommitted. Thus, a great deal of Canadian water is already subject to commercial claims, either because it has been allocated to various users or because it is subject to proprietary claims such as the rights of licensees and riparian users.[47]

Furthermore, as many other commentators have noted, water is a "good" under NAFTA and GATT rules because it is explicitly included under GATT tariff headings.[48] While the federal government has argued that this inclusion only concerns water that has been actually removed from its natural state—for example, water bottled for sale—the tariff schedules include no such limitation.

Finally on this particular subject, the much vaunted 1993 Statement upon which Canada has placed such great reliance does not on closer scrutiny appear to have much if any substance (see box). Even if it did, it would not alter the substantive provisions of NAFTA, a point the U.S. clearly made in acknowledging the release of the 1993 Statement.[49]

The Agreement That Never Was

The "three-Party" agreement that Canada has repeatedly pointed to as proof that both the U.S. and Mexico support Canada's sovereign authority over water has much less substance than it has led Canadians to believe. In fact, this 1993 Statement is no more than an unsigned document, on blank paper, released as an attachment to a press statement issued by the Government of Canada on December 2, 1993. There is no indication that either government offered formal support for it. Yet approval by the U.S. Senate is required under the U.S. Constitution with respect to all international treaties. Given the rather startling degree of informality that surrounds this 1993 Statement, it is not certain that it would even rise to the status of a non-binding agreement under international law.

Water as an Investment and Service

The issue of whether water is a "good" for the purposes of NAFTA is obviously a matter of considerable importance. But, by focusing attention on water as a tradeable commodity, the federal government is ignoring the fact that under NAFTA, water is both an investment and service, even if it is not considered to be a "good." Indeed, Canada's most onerous trade obligations are found in the investment and services provisions of NAFTA and the WTO, not in the trade-in-goods provisions of these treaties. Moreover, by putting its powerful enforcement machinery at the disposal of countless foreign investors, NAFTA leaves Canadian water resources, and measures established to protect them, entirely vulnerable to foreign investor claims (see box).

It is important in this regard to recognize that neither the investment nor the service provisions of NAFTA are in any way restricted to the trade of goods. Therefore, whether or not water is a "good" or "product" is irrelevant to a determination of rights and obligations arising under NAFTA and WTO agreements concerning investment and services.[50] In fact, the federal government appears to have conceded this point with respect to investments by indicating:

> Chapter 11 does not prevent NAFTA Parties from prohibiting the removal of water from its natural state. But foreign investors seeking to establish investment, or with established investments, for the removal of water from its natural state would have to be treated in the accordance with the obligations of the Chapter (such as national treatment, minimum standard of treatment and the four requirements for an expropriation, if there is one).

In other words, NAFTA investment disciplines apply to Canadian water resources, including access rights to Canadian water in its natural state.[51] This means that, once governments allow water to be withdrawn from its natural state, as they have on innumerable occasions for purposes that range from large-scale industrial use to personal consumption, the same rights must now be accorded foreign investors.

While the federal government remains silent on the issue of whether water would be subject to the services provisions of NAFTA and the WTO, for similar reasons, that result is also inescapable. This arguably means that a water services provider operating in Canada would have the same rights to apply water services to U.S. consumers as to Canadians.

There are several differences between the services rules set out in NAFTA and the General Agreement on Trade in Services (the GATS is discussed in more detail in the Chapter on Health). However, for water export controls one difference is particularly noteworthy because, under the GATS, the resources conservation exception set out under GATT Article XX(g) was explicitly deleted from the list of justifications for departing from the requirements of this particular trade agreement.

In other words, no matter how necessary it may be to conserve natural resources, Canada cannot interfere with the cross-border supply of services with respect to which full GATS obligations apply. To date, however, Canada has made no explicit commitment under the GATS with respect to water treatment or supply. But, because water is used to support so many of the services to which GATS disciplines do apply, the extent to which water may have already been caught by the web of constraints imposed by this WTO Agreement is uncertain.

Sun Belt Water

Sun Belt Water Inc. of Santa Barbara, California, is one of several U.S.-based corporations that have expressed an interest in exporting Canadian water in bulk. To date, however, it is the only one to claim damages because a Canadian government has refused to issue it a water export permit. Invoking the investor-state suit mechanism of NAFTA, Sun Belt is seeking several hundreds of millions of dollars in damages arising from B.C.'s actions to ban fresh-water exports under its Water Protection Act.

It argues that Canada is obliged under trade rules to issue it an export permit, or compensate it for the profits it would have made had such an approval been forthcoming. No doubt it is encouraged by a recent ruling compensating a U.S. hazardous waste disposal company denied a permit to operate by a local municipality in Mexico.[52]

A Citizen's Agenda

If our federal government were serious about protecting water, there are several steps that it would take to preserve its sovereign authority over this vital resource. These would include:

1. *Federal Legislation to Ban Water Exports*

The best federal approach for preventing bulk water removals from Canada is the enactment of federal legislation designed specifically for this purpose. In fact, such legislation is essential if water protection objectives are to be realized. However, for reasons noted, no matter how carefully designed, Canadian measures to prevent bulk water exports or diversion projects would still be vulnerable to trade challenges and/or investor-state claims.

2. *Exempting Water Under NAFTA and the WTO*

Therefore, once water export controls are in place, the next step would be for Canada to negotiate international measures to both strengthen these domestic initiatives and avert the risk of trade challenges and investor claims to them. First, Canada should negotiate an exclusion, exception or waiver for water export controls from the constraints imposed by NAFTA and the WTO. Second, Canada should also negotiate an international agreement concerning water that would explicitly supersede Canadian trade and investment obligations and take precedence in the event of conflicts with them.

The most problematic conflicts between water export controls and Canadian trade and investment commitments arise under, and are unique to, NAFTA. While the general prohibition against export controls established by GATT Article XI is problematic, WTO rules allow the imposition of export taxes on water resources, as NAFTA does not. More to the point, however, because pressure on Canadian water resources is most likely to come from the U.S., the availability of effective safeguard measures under the WTO is of little avail in attempting to protect Canadian water resources from U.S. claims. For these reasons, efforts to protect water from trade agreement based claims should be firmly fixed on NAFTA.

In this regard, the very broad exception established under Article 2102 with respect to National Security provides a useful prototype. To paraphrase and expand slightly upon the terms of this Article, this exception would provide that:

Nothing in this Agreement shall be construed to prevent or in any other way limit a Party from taking any action that it considers necessary for the protection or conservation of water in any form, including:

- relating to the extraction or trade of water for export or by diversion; or,

- relating to the implementation of national policies or international agreements respecting the conservation or protection of water.

Furthermore, any action taken by a Party in furtherance of these objectives will not be subject to the dispute settlement provisions of this Agreement.

3. An International Agreement on Water Sovereignty

Finally, to more firmly establish Canadian sovereignty with respect to water, it is also important that Canada negotiate a bilateral agreement with the U.S. concerning water conservation that would explicitly recognize the sovereign authority of both Canada and the U.S. to ban, embargo or tax water exports, in whatever form, or mode of withdrawal.

That treaty should include a clause asserting the paramountcy of its provisions should conflicts arise with other international agreements including those concerning trade, investment and services. While plans to amend the Boundary Water Treaties Act represent a step in this direction, the BWTA applies only to certain Canadian waters, does not engender a meaningful enforcement regime, and would not prevail should conflicts arise with NAFTA or WTO rules.[53]

Unfortunately, the course of action that prudence dictates Canada take to protect its water resources from unconstrained export demands, stands in sharp contrast to the approach adopted by the federal government.

It is discouraging that the federal government appears willing to abandon its responsibilities as steward of Canadian water resources rather than seek amendments to the trade agreements that it now concedes drastically limit its options to do so. Instead, it is attempting to finesse those trade constraints by adopting a strategy that is very unlikely to survive a trade challenge of foreign investor claim.

7

Energy

When it comes to trade in energy resources, the provisions of NAFTA are far more important for Canada than those found in the WTO Agreements. This is the case because NAFTA provisions go much further in reducing the scope for government regulation of international energy trade, and include three important trade provisions that cannot be found under the WTO. These NAFTA rules have such far-reaching implications for North American energy development that they deserve at least a brief description.

NAFTA Revisited

The first is the proportional sharing provision of NAFTA which entitles the U.S. to a proportional share of Canadian energy resources in perpetuity, or until those resources are entirely exhausted.[54] The exact proportion of Canadian resources to which the U.S. can lay claim is equal to the relative share being exported at the time that export constraints are imposed—or, in other words, by the unregulated market. There is no equivalent rule in any of the WTO agreements, and in fact this proportional sharing clause does not apply between the U.S. and our other NAFTA partner, Mexico.

The second unique feature of NAFTA rules for energy trade prohibits the imposition of export taxes that exceed those applicable to domestic consumption.[55] In contrast, WTO rules allow countries to establish two-price energy or resource policies. When coupled with the quantitative control prohibitions of GATT Article XI,[56] this ban on export taxation effectively and entirely removes government control of energy exports.

The third significant departure from generally applicable trade rules that is found in NAFTA exempts government subsidies for oil and gas exploration and development from trade challenge.[57] Again, nothing in the WTO Agreement on Subsidies or in any other WTO agreement resembles this astonishing inducement to use public funds to support the extravagant fossil fuel appetites that Canada and the U.S. share.

Global Trade's Energy Appetite

This is not to say, however, that WTO rules are not important to energy trade. They are, and for several reasons. To begin with, all GATT rules relating to trade in goods also apply to energy resources trade, and, as we have seen, these rules impose serious constraints on government regulatory options for environmental and resource conservation purposes. However, the most important energy-related impacts of WTO rules are probably those that arise from the enormous transportation demands of a global economy.

In fact, the entire edifice of global production and trade depends in large measure on an unlimited supply of cheap energy required to move an ever-increasing international flow of goods and materials. If it were not for the capacity to externalize a large share of the true costs associated with energy use (e.g., the costs associated with climate change), the carbon-based model of globalization which now dominates would soon unravel under the enormous real costs of moving more and more materials and goods, longer and longer distances.

As noted, the globalization of agricultural production and trade has and will continue to increase the energy intensity of agricultural production and distribution. And it is important to note again that food systems are arguably the world's largest industry, and likely its largest user of fossil fuels. Exposing this critical relationship between agricultural policies and energy use provides a compelling illustration of the importance of developing a much broader and holistic strategy for confronting such problems as global warming.

It is also revealing of the enormity of the problems that can result from failing to integrate environmental analysis with economic, industrial, and resource policies. Unfortunately, no government has been willing to submit its trade policies to a meaningful environmental assessment. It is obviously critical for them to do so.

A Carbon Tax as a Border Tax Adjustment

The WTO regime also has considerable potential to affect efforts to implement carbon or energy taxes as part of a strategy to reduce greenhouse-gas emissions. The Framework Convention on Climate Change contemplates the use of energy charges or taxes as tools for combatting global warming. Given the multitude of causes that have given rise to excessive greenhouse-gas emissions, it seems inevitable that such taxes will have to play an important role if reduction goals are to be achieved.

Because of its pervasive impact on most industrial inputs and processes, a significant carbon tax could have a substantial impact on the international competitiveness of many sectors of the economy. Over the long term, there is probably no better prescription for a competitive economy than forcing it to become a more efficient user of energy and other resources. Over the short term, however, significant price disadvantages can be created for domestic producers by increasing energy costs in the absence of international agreements to implement similar increases for foreign competitors. It is these competitiveness impacts that currently stand as an important impediment to the implementation of such tax regimes.[58]

It is apparent, then, that if the use of energy taxes is to become feasible, governments must find effective ways to ensure that such measures do not confront domestic producers with the choice of either going out of business or moving to the nearest pollution haven. One obvious way to ameliorate the adverse trade impacts of a carbon tax would be to apply import taxes and/or export rebates to level the playing field between domestic and foreign producers.

Under WTO rules, the imposition of such taxes might be authorized under the heading of "border tax adjustments" as defined in Articles II, 2(a) and III, 2 of the GATT agreement. A GATT working group that explored the meaning of these trade provisions adopted the following definition for such measures:

> any fiscal measure which puts into effect, in whole or in part, the destination principle (i.e., which enables exported products to be relieved of some or all of the tax charged in the exporting country in respect of similar domestic products sold to consumers on the home market, and which enables imported products sold to consumers to be charged with some or all of the tax charged in the importing country in respect of similar domestic products).[59]

In addition, under these GATT rules, governments can impose border tax adjustments not only on goods, but also on the materials used to make these goods.

What all of this means for a prospective carbon tax is this: governments can impose import taxes on energy goods, if the same tax is applied to energy goods produced locally and sold into domestic markets. Conversely, a government is free to provide a tax rebate on energy goods sold on international markets which equals the tax applied to the same goods sold to domestic consumers. From an environmental perspective, this option makes sense only when energy exports are destined for a jurisdiction with a reciprocal system of import taxation.

These same border measures could also be applied to goods that incorporate energy products, such as plastics. In this case, the border tax adjustment would reflect the value of the energy contained in the product, not the value of the product itself. So far, so good. The problem arises, however, with respect to the treatment of taxes that relate to energy inputs that are not incorporated in the final product, e.g., energy used to harvest, extract, transport, produce, process, and package the product.

For most products, these tax effects will have the largest impact on product price. Here trade rules raise serious problems and, according to the GATT Working Group that considered this issue, the use of border tax adjustments to address the competitiveness impacts of taxes on energy and other inputs remains unresolved.

To illustrate the potential problems that would confront such an initiative, consider the use of a border tax measure that was intended to reflect the energy used to transport goods to market. Such a border tax adjustment would necessarily discriminate against goods that must travel further. From an environmental perspective, this is precisely the signal that a carbon tax should provide, but from a trade perspective such a measure would offend the "national treatment" requirements of GATT Article III to treat "like goods" in a like manner.

As we have seen, according to trade panel rulings, no distinctions may be made between products having the same physical characteristics. In this way, and as we have seen, trade rules force governments and consumers to ignore the enormous differences that may exist between identical products when account is taken of the environmental impacts associated with their production and transportation.

Therefore, if a carbon tax border adjustment is to be considered consistent with WTO restraints, it is imperative that a much broader definition be given to "like product" so that account can be taken of all environmental impacts of making and moving that product. This would give governments and consumers the power to favour those products that reflect environmentally sound production, and to discriminate against products that fail to meet sustainable standards. There should only be two relevant trade conditions that would potentially restrict such import or export taxes:

- Is the measure part of a *bona fide* domestic program intended to accomplish environmental objectives? And

- Is the calculation of the border tax adjustment a reasonable estimate of the taxes that would be applied to goods produced locally, and for domestic markets?

A Citizen's Agenda

Pending such interpretations, it is incumbent on governments to ensure that real or perceived trade impediments do not stall much-needed action to address pressing ecological problems. For example, parties to the Climate Change Convention need to make clear their intention to have the provisions of the Convention prevail in the case of conflict with WTO rules. They can accomplish that goal by declaring that intention as part of any Protocol they may negotiate.

Similarly, should such a multilateral consensus not quickly emerge, it will be important for governments, particularly in countries with extravagant energy habits such as Canada, to proceed on their own with domestic measures needed to reduce greenhouse-gas emissions. If needed to address the competitive disadvantages that such measures might create, border tax adjustments could be levied on the premise that a *bona fide* measure will be sustained by the WTO if a trade dispute arises.

Should such measures raise concerns for our trading partners, then we will simply have to address them. In that process we will contribute to the ultimate narrowing of the chasm that currently divides environmental and trade policy. Simply conceding the primacy of trade rules, without even testing them, is not a feasible response in light of the potentially catastrophic consequences of inaction.

8

Environmental Standards and Other Technical Barriers to Trade

This guide attempts throughout to integrate an environmental perspective as part of a critique of all aspects of the WTO regime. Here the focus is on the most obvious ways in which trade and environmental agendas intersect: the impact of WTO rules on environmental standards. There are many ways in which trade rules limit options for establishing regulatory initiatives for environmental or conservation purposes. The following assessment highlights the more important points of contradiction between trade rules and environmental policy goals.

Subsidizing Competitiveness at the Expense of the Environment

Under the WTO Agreement on Subsidies and Countervailing Measures, governments are not to subsidize domestic producers in ways that enhance their competitiveness internationally. Such subsidies are regarded as distorting true competition, and are therefore at odds with the free market model. Some subsidies are prohibited under this WTO Agreement, while others are "actionable" and may justify the imposition of counter-measures (e.g., countervailing duties) by a country whose producers are adversely affected by the subsidy.

Over the years, trade rules have been used on numerous occasions to challenge a wide variety of government programs and practices as unfair subsidies. However, trade officials have been steadfast in resisting the notion that the absence of environmental regulations be treated as an unfair subsidy, and no trade complaint has ever raised this challenge.

Nevertheless, it is demonstrable that the absence of environmental or resource conservation regulations can make domestic producers more competitive in both domestic and international markets. Because such producers are free to externalize the environmental costs of production, they are in a very real sense being subsidized at public expense. It should not matter that the currency of that subsidy is a public natural resource, such as a national forest, or a community's clean air or water, rather than a public fiscal resource, tax revenue.

In fact, as the Raw Log-Export case illustrates, trade panels have not had great difficulty accepting rather ingenious arguments about government regulations (export controls) conferring indirect, but actionable subsidies (see case study in Chapter VI). Yet no government has initiated a trade complaint to challenge another jurisdiction that has neglected or abandoned environmental regulation in order to attract or keep investment. Because trade complaints are almost always made at the urging of corporations, it is understandable that no country has been keen to challenge government inaction on the environmental regulatory front.

Because environmental regulation can often represent a significant cost of doing business, corporations often weigh the presence of such regulations as a significant factor when deciding where to establish operations. Therefore, when trade rules ignore the competitiveness effects of absent environmental regulation, governments are encouraged to compete for investment by offering to become havens for polluters. Conversely, companies are free to whipsaw one jurisdiction against another in an effort to drive both down to the lowest common denominator of environmental protection.

Environmentalists have described the practice of exporting goods from pollution havens as "ecological dumping." Under Article VI of the GATT, dumping is "condemned" as the practice "by which products of one country are introduced into the commerce of another country at less than the normal value of the products," and normal value is defined as including "the cost of production." Thus, environmentalists have argued that exports from pollution havens are "dumped" onto international markets at prices below the real costs of production, the difference in price being the value of environmental externalities—polluted air and water. Notwithstanding Article VI, however, GATT officials have been no more receptive to this argument than they have been to the notion that absent environmental regulations be considered subsidies.

The Big Chill

Most environmental regulatory initiatives are opposed, often vigorously, by corporations that would be subject to such new laws. At times, opposition is motivated by a desire to avoid the costs of pollution prevention or control technologies. On other occasions, it is the cost of environmental liability insurance or reporting requirements that are targets for corporate lobbyists. Even where the environmental program will ultimately reduce the costs of production or actually improve competitiveness over time, efforts to head off new regulations are often just as determined.

Whether the costs of environmental regulation are real or merely perceived, they are inevitably front and centre when business groups lobby governments about environmental law reform. A ubiquitous feature of these efforts is the claim that the costs of environmental regulation will put the industry at a competitive disadvantage and even force it to relocate or close. These are claims that are notoriously difficult for governments to evaluate, because it is usually impossible for public officials to assess their validity. For these reasons, threats of disinvestment or capital flight have always been potent weapons in the arsenal of corporate lobbyists seeking to defeat regulatory initiatives.

In the new global economy, where corporations can establish or relocate operations and trade freely throughout the world, arguments about the costs of regulation have been made significantly more powerful. For reluctant politicians and public officials, trade constraints (often more perceived than real), become the convenient excuse for not tabling environmental initiatives at all. Thus the overall impact of this WTO spectre hovering in the shadows is to cast a chill over prospective environmental regulations. It is no coincidence that, since the advent of free trade regimes, environmentalists now spend as much time defending existing laws as they do fighting for new ones.

The Technical Barriers to Trade (TBT) Agreement

While the absence of environmental regulation is off limits under the WTO regime, the existence of environmental and other "technical regulations" are considered matters that must be closely scrutinized. That is why an entire WTO Agreement on environmental and other standards—the Agreement on Technical Barriers to Trade—was deemed necessary to ensure that no "non-tariff barriers" interfere, even indirectly, with trade liberalization goals. It is, of course, telling of the purpose of this WTO agreement that it defines environmental laws as technical barriers to trade.

From the perspective of transnational corporations, if environmental regulations must be endured, it is critical to the viability of global production and trade that such standards are homogeneous from one jurisdiction to another. Thus, the essential thrusts of the TBT Agreement are two-fold: first, to create substantial impediments to the introduction of environmental regulations; and, second, to force the international harmonization of environmental regulation when public demand for these measures cannot be resisted.

Under Article 2.4 of the TBT Agreement, where international standards have been established, governments that can demonstrate the need for regulatory initiatives are directed to ensure that their own regulations conform to them. Also under these TBT rules, regulations that implement international standards are presumed to be in compliance with WTO rules. Even in this case, however, other countries are free to invoke dispute resolution under the WTO to challenge such environmental measures. Thus, even where an international consensus exists, governments must still be prepared to demonstrate that their particular environmental standard is both "necessary" and "the least trade-restrictive" way to achieve the conservation or environmental goal it is trying to accomplish. It needs also to be noted that in most areas of environmental regulation no international consensus or standard exists.

As trade dispute panels have interpreted these requirements, this burden of proof has become so onerous that no environmental initiative has ever survived the challenge. There is now a growing list of such casualties, ranging from marine mammal protection laws to food safety standards. (See the case studies included in this guide.)

Creating a Ceiling but No Floor for Environmental Regulation

While the TBT Agreement requires no minimal level of environmental regulation—and in fact discourages it—it does create very substantial obstacles for governments that want to regulate where no international standard exists, or go further than international norms. For governments that have the courage to proceed in these circumstances, onerous administrative hurdles must be overcome.

These include the duty to: notify other WTO members of its initiative; provide copies and supporting documentation when requested; provide an opportunity for comment: and demonstrate how those comments have been taken into account.[60] It is noteworthy that these obligations to provide other WTO members (and their resident corporations) with a right to notice and comment are mandatory, even though these same rights will often not be available to local citizens.

After complying with these requirements, a government still intent on proceeding with an initiative must then provide "a reasonable interval" so foreign producers can adapt to new requirements. Moreover, the TBT Agreement extends these obligations to cover provincial regulatory initiatives, and even seeks to bind some municipal and even non-governmental measures, as well. The administrative costs associated with these obligations alone will often be enough to discourage would-be regulators, and they are certainly beyond the capacity of all but the most affluent nations. Nevertheless, failure to comply with these procedures is itself grounds for trade challenge.

Following the Leader

Because international standards require a consensus among governments, they invariably reflect a compromise between nations persuaded of the need for tough environmental standards and those which are not. But under TBT rules, this lower common denominator becomes the *de facto* ceiling for all national initiatives. Furthermore, by trying to make international consensus the effective precondition to regulation, the TBT Agreement threatens the underlying "follow the leader" dynamic of law reform which has for years provided a critical impetus to regulatory reform and initiative.

According to this dynamic, as soon as one jurisdiction is persuaded to blaze a trail, others are then encouraged to follow. In this way environmentalists can point to California's auto exhaust standards, Sweden's air pollution laws for waste incinerators, Ontario's curbside recycling programs, or Germany's packaging laws as demonstrable evidence that tougher environmental laws are possible and practical. This disturbing effect of WTO harmonization rules is to stop, or substantially slow down, jurisdictions that might otherwise be willing to establish international precedents.

For corporations that oppose environmental regulation, the importance of preventing the trend-setting initiative is well understood, as the following case study illustrates.

Canadian Asbestos Exports

In 1989, the U.S. Environmental Protection Agency announced that it was introducing regulations to phase out the production, import, and use of asbestos. The ban was the culmination of more than 10 years of struggle that had involved several Congressional investigations and thousands of lives.[61] The EPA estimated that the ban on this cancer-causing material could save 1,900 lives by the turn of the century.[62] But no sooner was the program announced than it was angrily denounced as insincere and politically motivated. Leading the charge was the government of Quebec, which has a substantial stake in asbestos mining. A Quebec labour leader went so far as to warn other countries "not be duped by the phoney concerns" of the U.S. administration.[63]

Intervening to assert the interests of the Quebec asbestos mining industry, the government of Canada joined in a legal challenge to the U.S. EPA initiative. In its brief to the U.S. Court of Appeals, Canada argued that the U.S. asbestos regulations violated its obligations under GATT and FTA. Repeating the proscriptions of international trade agreements, Canada argued that, because the EPA had banned asbestos when no international scientific consensus supported the need to do so, it must therefore be taken to have done so for trade protection reasons rather than for a legitimate domestic objective.

Even more significant, however, was the motive that inspired Canada's challenge to regulations in a jurisdiction that did not represent an important market for Canadian asbestos exports. As explained by the Minister of Mines for the Province of Quebec:

> (The) biggest fear is that other countries will follow the U.S. example. The European Community... could, following the U.S. decision, adopt analogous regulations. We also fear the impact of the EPA decision on development projects in countries receiving American economic aid.[64]

The U.S. Court of Appeals ultimately upheld the challenge to the EPA ban on the grounds that the Agency had rejected alternatives less burdensome to the industry, and failed to observe proper rule-making procedures.

More recently, similar concerns have been expressed by Canada and Quebec about the decision by the French government last year to follow the lead of several other European nations and implement a ban on the use of asbestos. Again Canada was quick to respond by launching a campaign to persuade the French government to reconsider its decision.[65] In fact, the federal government is funding these efforts to ensure that European initiatives do not spread to the developing countries that represent Quebec's most important export market for this hazardous and carcinogenic substance.[66]

When those efforts failed, Canada decided in late 1998 to invoke WTO dispute resolution in a bid to defeat France's regulatory initiative. The case has yet to be resolved.

Thus, the TBT Agreement sets out detailed rules for eliminating any constraint that regulatory initiatives might create for free trade. In doing so, it consistently betrays an indifference to the administrative, economic, social, and political realities of environmental regulation. As do all other elements of the WTO regime, it unquestioningly assumes the priority of trade policy objectives, even when on rare occasions it reveals some awareness that other public policy objectives might exist.

The First WTO Trade Ruling

The following case study has been reserved until this point because of its complexity. However, given the fact that the very first case to be resolved under WTO rules involved a successful challenge to an important environmental program, it seems appropriate to describe the trade panel ruling in some detail. While it repeats many of the conclusions of earlier trade panel decisions concerning environmental or conservation initiatives, it is unfortunately likely to be given greater weight in light of having the benefit of the WTO imprimatur.

Reformulated Gasoline

In the first decision to be handed down by the WTO,[67] U.S. Clean Air regulations were ruled to be inconsistent with WTO rules, and the U.S. was "requested" to amend its regulations or face retaliatory trade sanctions, in the order of $150 million per year. At issue in this landmark case were regulations developed by the U.S. Environmental Protection Agency for tackling the serious air quality problems, including excessively high levels of ground level ozone, that prevail in certain areas of the U.S. As part of that strategy, the EPA developed regulations intended to reduce pollution by going after a primary cause of air quality problems: gasoline combustion.

Known as the "Gasoline Rule," these regulations established certain compositional and performance specifications intended to reduce emissions from gasoline combustion in "non-attainment" areas, where levels of pollution exceeded air quality objectives. In searching for an effective and economically feasible regulatory approach, the EPA had opted for a program that required gradual improvement based on past performance.[68] In this way, it had sought to create the flexibility needed to allow an orderly transition by domestic and foreign producers that would avoid supply disruptions and other economic distortions.

The difficulty of this approach lay in the requirement of determining reliable baseline levels for both domestic and foreign sources of gasoline products. To do so, various approaches were authorized for determining these baselines that reflected the degree to which information was available about the performance and composition of gasoline sold in the baseline year. Where reliable information was not available, the industry would have to sell gasoline no more contaminated than the industry average for 1990.

For corporations that could produce accurate records, a more precise determination was allowed. However, in light of the difficulties associated with trying to elicit accurate information from all of the potential foreign sources of U.S. gas imports, the Gasoline Rule held all imported gasoline to the 1990 industry average. As a result, some domestic and foreign producers were treated identically, some domestic producers were held to higher standards than foreign suppliers, and some to a lower one.

Predictably, some foreign refiners objected to the costs associated with upgrading their refineries in order to produce cleaner gasoline. Those corporations complained and prompted their governments to file a trade complaint taking issue with the methodology used by the EPA for establishing baseline performance. Thus, in early 1995, Brazil and Venezuela filed a formal trade complaint with the WTO claiming that their gasoline products were being held to a higher standard than was being applied to U.S. refiners.

The decision of the trade panel convened to hear the dispute, and subsequently of the WTO's Appellate Body (AB), was that U.S. Clean Air regulations were in violation of the national treatment provisions set out in Article III of GATT. Furthermore, the U.S. could not rely on the environmental and resource conservation exceptions set out in Article XX to sustain its regulatory approach.

Before getting into the details of the WTO panel's decision, an important preliminary point needs to be made. This is to underscore the fact that the regulations at issue in this case were not established to regulate gasoline trade, nor were they created to improve the competitive position of U.S. fuel refiners. Rather, the Clean Air Act initiative clearly represented a *bona fide* effort to address the serious air quality problems caused by gasoline combustion, particularly in regions of the country suffering from significant levels of air pollution. Whatever the impacts of these Clean Air Act regulations on foreign gas producers, it is undeniable that those effects were incidental to the environmental goals the EPA was endeavouring to achieve. It is important to keep this context in mind when considering the esoteric reasoning of the panel convened to hear this trade case.

Because the U.S. declined to appeal several of the findings of the panel, it is important to read that decision together with that of the AB. The first finding of the panel was that the EPA's Gasoline Rule violated GATT Article III, which requires all countries to treat imports no less favourably than "like" domestic products. This requirement of "national treatment" is, as we know, one of the cornerstones of GATT law. Thus, notwithstanding the fact that the Gasoline Rule was applied in precisely the same manner to at least some domestic producers, the panel had no difficulty in finding the U.S. to be in breach of Article III.

Having found this fundamental breach of GATT rules, the panel declined to consider a number of other potential violations that might also have spelled disaster for these Clean Air Act regulations. Once it had been found in breach of its obligations under GATT, it was then necessary for the U.S. to demonstrate that its regulations fell within one of the exceptions to GATT rules that are set out in Article XX, which provides in part:

General Exceptions

Subject to the requirement that such measures are not applied in a manner which would constitute a means of arbitrary or unjustifiable discrimination between countries where the same conditions prevail, or a disguised restriction on international trade, nothing in this Agreement shall be construed to prevent the adoption or enforcement by any contracting party of measures:

> *(b) necessary to protect human, animal or plant life or health;*
>
> *(g) relating to the conservation of exhaustible natural resources if such measures are made effective in conjunction with restrictions on domestic production or consumption.*

As to the application of these exceptions, both the decisions of the panel and the AB are quite lengthy and filled with convoluted and often contradictory reasoning. Deducing the common and essential conclusions from this murky logic is difficult, but some points clearly emerge. On the essential point, there was no disagreement: U.S. EPA regulations did not qualify for protection under Article XX exceptions. As to precisely why Article XX was of no avail, the panel and AB had a differing view.

According to the panel, to qualify under the umbrella created by Article XX (b), a country seeking to defend environmental or resource conservation measures as "necessary to protect human, animal or plant life health" must pass a three-fold test and establish:

1. that it had reviewed all reasonably available alternatives for accomplishing its environmental or resource policy objectives and determined that none was consistent with GATT provisions;

2. that it had "adequately" explored the possibility of negotiating multilateral agreements with all of its trading partners that might be affected by the regulatory initiative, in order to find some consensual resolution; and that, failing which,

3. it had chosen the least trade-restrictive measure for achieving its goals.

The panel concluded that these were tests the U.S. had failed to meet, and, as was true of the panel's ruling on violation of Article III, the U.S. chose not to appeal from these findings.

As for the requirements of Article XX(g), the panel and AB agreed that a party seeking to rely upon this exception must be able to demonstrate that its regulations were "primarily aimed at" the conservation of an exhaustible natural resource. On this point the AB parted company with the panel and found that the Gasoline Rule did meet this criterion. However, it then went on to find that, in any event, Article XX(g) was of no avail in this case because the Gasoline Rule failed to meet the additional burden of satisfying the requirements engendered by the preamble to Article XX.

Moreover, in reading the preamble as imposing burdens additional to those set out in the subparagraphs, the AB actually imported the "necessity" test used to evaluate XX(b) claims. In the result, the rigour of proving "necessity" now qualifies recourse to any of the sub-categories of Article XX, even though no other sub-paragraph actually articulates this threshold requirement.

Finally, the AB concluded that, in order to satisfy the requirements expressed in the preamble to Article XX, a country must also be able to demonstrate that it has taken into account the cost of compliance for all foreign producers that may be affected by its regulations.

As is now the practice of dispute panels in these cases, both panel and AB members had no hesitation in second-guessing environmental officials on the details of complex administrative, economic, and policy matters related to their regulatory agendas. Neither did they have any reluctance to articulate ill-defined, subjective, and open-ended criteria such as "least trade-restrictive" or "reasonably available" alternatives as the necessary preconditions for compliance with Article XX. Nor did they hesitate to impose administrative burdens, such as determining the cost of compliance for foreign corporations, that are clearly impossible to meet.

As preposterous as these interpretations are from an environmental policy perspective, they are almost as questionable from the perspective of judicial interpretation. Often guilty of logically flawed reasoning that ignores the plain meaning of GATT provisions, trade dispute bodies have established compliance tests and other obligations without any textual support whatsoever from the WTO provisions. For example, there is nothing in Article XX or in any other GATT provision that speaks of the need to seek international agreement in order to establish that a *bona fide* environmental regulation represents a justifiable exception to GATT strictures.

Neither is there any GATT language to support several of the other tests that trade panels have devised to determine whether a measure is "primarily aimed" at conservation, or that it is the "least trade-restrictive" of "reasonably available alternatives." Nor have the trade panels that have enunciated these tests felt under any obligation to reveal the authority upon which they relied in developing them.

In consequence, if an environmental or resource conservation regulation is to survive the gauntlet of a trade-dispute challenge, it must be able to negotiate its way through a shifting minefield of highly subjective criteria and tests. Moreover, the absence of consistent or logically sound interpretation has meant that the trip must be taken blindfolded. It is very difficult to imagine any environmental initiative surviving this challenge—and in fact none have.

After all of this, then, it is important to remember that what was at stake here was the right of foreign gas refiners to export to the U.S. gasoline that is more contaminated than the 1990 industry average. The costs of this victory for trade policy goals will be measured in increased levels of ground level ozone and other hazardous air pollutants, and with these the respiratory distress and elevated mortality rates associated with these pollutants. The other casualty is the enormous investment of time, resources and political capital that were needed to establish this regulatory regime in the first place, and that must now be arduously repeated.

A Citizen's Agenda

As the case notes reproduced here reveal, governments at the behest of large corporations have increasingly resorted to trade challenges to assail environmental and resource conservation initiatives. Unfortunately, the TBT and SPS Agreements have provided substantial new grounds upon which to launch such complaints. It is clear that the establishment of these trade rules represents a significant step backwards for environmental protection and resource conservation. It is imperative, then, to expose the environmental consequences of these trade rules, in order to bring about the fundamental reforms that are needed.

It is at least somewhat helpful that both the TBT and SPS Agreements speak of the rights of countries to pursue "legitimate domestic objectives," including the "protection of human health or safety, animal plant life or health, or the environment." If these provisions were to be given broad reading, they would provide some scope for sovereign and democratic decision-making when it comes to public health and environmental protection. Unfortunately, however, as we have seen, the interpretation that has been given to similar terms in GATT Article XX has rendered this language all but meaningless. Governments, therefore, must now rewrite WTO rules to restore their environmental policy and regulatory prerogatives.

Finally, it should be noted that, under Canada's constitutional arrangements, provincial governments have important powers to deal with environmental protection and conservation matters. Accordingly, it is not within the federal government's constitutional authority to unilaterally usurp provincial jurisdiction by simply signing an international trade agreement that undermines or negates provincial prerogatives. Provinces must therefore stand their constitutional ground and reject the purported constraints imposed by WTO rules by freely exercising their constitutional mandates to legislate on behalf of their constituents.

9

Workers' Rights

The advent of free trade a decade ago represented a fundamental departure from the trade policies that had framed the economic strategies of most nations for much of this century. Import substitution, regional economic development programs, supply management for agricultural commodities and other similar policies had established an important role for government in fostering economic development through tariffs and various import and export controls.

While international trade was a vital part of domestic economic policy, it was not considered paramount to the interests of local businesses or workers. Trade in resources, agricultural commodities, and manufactured goods was carefully regulated by government to ensure that it primarily served the interests of their constituents.

Perhaps the best example of what these policies meant for Canadian workers can be found in the the Canada–U.S. Automobile Trade Agreement (the Auto Pact), negotiated in 1965. The Auto Pact established the basis for the development of the automobile industry in Canada through its one simple principle: if U.S. auto-makers wanted to sell cars in Canada, they would have to build them here. This "site here to sell here" approach is the antithesis of free trade, and the Auto Pact represented a very tangible example of a viable and modern approach to regulating trade that serves the interests of both Canadian and U.S. workers.

Indeed, the Auto Pact endured for so many years, in part because it was sheltered from the full impact of free trade rules, but also because of the enormous capital infrastructure and integrated production systems that it was responsible for establishing in central Canada and the American Midwest. Today, it accounts for a large percentage of the remaining manufacturing strength of Canada's economy, and is the largest manufacturing sector in Ontario. Because of its success, the Auto Pact stood as a symbol of the success of trade regulation. It is this prominence that probably explains the antipathy with which it was regarded by the Canadian business press that advocated its abolition.[69]

Yet, when the proponents of free trade boast about trade figures with the United States in order to prove the virtues of free trade for Canadian manufacturers, they conveniently forget to mention that the single largest contributor is the auto industry, where exports are part of an approach to trade regulation that they would have us abandon.

With the establishment of free trade regimes, we have all but lost the means by which jobs in the auto industry and many other sectors have been created and sustained. (Because of its importance, and because of the recent WTO ruling against this trade agreement, we will consider the Auto Pact in detail later in this chapter.)

How do we describe the profound impact that free trade is having on working people? We'll begin by examining the theoretical arguments in favour of free trade and then track how that theory has been expressed in the rules of international trade, with particular emphasis on the role of tariffs, subsidies, services, and investment agreements. We will then look at organized labour's response to these challenges and assess the merits and pitfalls associated with including a "labour rights" clause in the WTO.

We must note at the outset that the impacts of free trade policies on working people are pervasive, from declining health care services to stagnating wages and job losses. We have described many of these adverse impacts elsewhere as we examined the impact of trade de-regulation on employment in the natural resource sectors, in agriculture, or in consequence of establishing international investment treaties such as the MAI. In this chapter we broaden our focus to look at how trade liberalization fundamentally reduces the capacity of working people to organize unions, negotiate reasonable terms of employment, find jobs, or demand reasonable compensation for work if they find it.

Free Trade Orthodoxy: Quoting Adam Smith Out of Context

The radical transformation of the basic architecture of national trade policies rests on a very shaky theoretical foundation: the principle of "comparative advantage." According to this 19th-century theory, credited to Adam Smith and David Ricardo, international trade operates to foster "win-win" outcomes for all who participate. By encouraging countries to specialize in doing those things only they do best, prosperity is assured for all.

There are, however, several shortcomings to this theory, including the pitfalls of ignoring the importance of diversity to the viability of any economy. The folly of putting all of our eggs in one basket is as obvious as it is alien to the logic of ever-increasing corporate growth and concentration.

But the most fundamental flaw of the new orthodoxy is that it conveniently ignores the issue of capital mobility. For, essential to Ricardo's and Smith's theory of comparative advantage was that capital would be rooted in particular nations.[70] Both men recognized that their theory would not work within nations, because the free movement of capital within national borders would mean that investment was governed not by comparative advantage, but by absolute profitability.[71]

This critical premise appears to have been forgotten by contemporary economists who espouse the virtues of comparative advantage in a world in which large amounts of capital move around the world every day with the speed of electronic impulse. If one is looking for intellectual rigour, it will have to be found elsewhere than in the theoretical underpinings of free trade orthodoxy, which rests on a profound misrepresentation of first principles.

> "I sympathize, therefore, with those who would minimize economic entanglement between nations. Ideas, knowledge, art, hospitality, travel—these are the things which should of their nature be international. But let goods be homespun whenever it is reasonably possible; and above all let finance be primarily national."
> —J.M. Keynes

In the real world, sophisticated telecommunications and management technologies give corporations unprecedented flexibility in organizing production and distribution systems. Unfettered capital mobility and free trade allow corporations to move or establish production anywhere. Consequently, corporations use their mobility to encourage competition among nations to provide more and more favourable conditions for investment. Governments are thus reduced to competing for investment by shedding minimum-wage laws, reducing environmental and labour standards, and abandoning any hope of taxing corporations to support basic infrastructure and services.

In reality, "comparative advantage" is a smoke-screen to mask a less palatable reality: free trade policies predominantly serve the interests of large trading corporations. Indeed, when the mobility of capital is taken into account, the edifice of free trade theory collapses, revealing the faulty assumption upon which it is based. Trade between two nations no longer serves their mutual economic interest; in fact, it may impoverish both. The comparative advantage of nations in the free trade context becomes the absolute advantage of corporations.

To be sure, this has brought considerable prosperity to those closely associated with the corporate sphere; but for most workers, free trade has meant job losses, job insecurity, unsafe working conditions, declining social services, and stagnating wages. We will consider the particular circumstances of Canadian workers under free trade below; but first we should briefly describe those elements of the free trade agenda that have the greatest impact on working people.

The general architecture of the GATT, National Treatment, and Most Favoured Nation Treatment undermine the capacity of governments to establish domestic economic development programs. The Technical Barriers to Trade Agreement, which we discuss in Chapter 7, has a direct impact on workplace health and safety regulation. As well, four other aspects of the WTO regime have particular importance for workers. The first, impacts of international investment agreements, is discussed in Chapter 11. Here we consider the other three: tariffs, subsidies, and services.

Tariffs and Jobs

We noted earlier that international trade agreements such as the Auto Pact engender policies that are fundamentally antithetical to the principles of free trade. Until it was recently struck down by the WTO, the Auto Pact offered a prime example of how the use of trade regulation, in this case import tariffs, can foster economic development. Thus, the capacity of governments to impose tariffs on foreign products creates the leverage needed to force investment in local production as a condition of access to markets or resources. In other words, the ability to restrict access to local markets or resources by imposing import or export tariffs, becomes the bargaining chip governments can use to force local investment.

In this regard, there is an absolutely critical distinction between NAFTA and the trade agreements in place under the WTO. In the latter, tariff measures are permitted for most traded goods and commodities. While WTO rules impose far-reaching constraints on the capacity of governments to regulate even within the domestic context (see, for example, the WTO agreements on intellectual property rights), the opportunity to use tariffs still represents a powerful tool for achieving domestic economic policy goals. Under NAFTA, however, with very few exceptions (the Auto Pact being one, although these tariffs are to be phased out), Canada has agreed to abandon the use of tariffs, whether on exports of raw commodities, to encourage value-added processing,[72] or on imports of manufactured goods, to encourage local production and investment.

It would be difficult to overstate the importance of this difference between these two trade regimes. Moreover, understanding this distinction is crucial to mobilizing opposition to the removal of tariff powers that is part of the current WTO agenda. This is taking place in the context of tariff-reduction negotiations for various industrial sectors which, like other trade negotiations, are taking place behind closed doors. Because tariffs are one of the most important means by which governments can regulate corporate activity for public policy purposes, it is vital that these prerogatives be vigorously defended.

It is encouraging, therefore, that at least one set of tariffs negotiations—for forest products—has provoked a vigorous response from forest activists concerned about the added pressure tariff reductions will exert on already overstressed forest resources. The ensuing debate has brought much-needed public attention to these important discussions. Similar light must now be cast on other sectoral tariff negotiations. For Canada, the challenge will also be to extricate itself from the constraints imposed by NAFTA. A determined resistance to tariff elimination in the WTO would be a vital first step.

Subsidies and Economic Development

There are other important regulatory, fiscal, and programmatic tools that can be used by governments to encourage and support domestic economic development. These include funding for research and development, joint ventures, education and job training, tax relief, loan guarantees, procurement contracts, and direct financial support in the form of subsidies. WTO rules significantly limit the use of most of these measures.

Consider, for example, the impact of WTO rules on the abililty of governments to use subsidies. For many decades, Canada has used subsidy programs to foster regional economic development. More recently, it has turned to the use of subsidies (and other program supports) to foster economic development in high-tech industrial sectors, such as telecomunications and aerospace.

As we have noted in our discussion of agricultural subsidies, the use of public fiscal resources to support unsustainable economic activity is very problematic. Under NAFTA, protection is provided for subsidies to support oil and gas exploration and development, and defence spending. The reshaping of Canadian economic development strategies in accordance with these new constraints has obvious and disturbing implications.

However, government support for sustainable forms of economic development is vital. Nowhere is this more apparent than for technological innovations that will allow us to meet pressing ecological challenges. Fuel-efficiency technologies such as fuel cells, eco-forestry alternatives to clear-cut logging, alternative fibre sources for paper, soil conservation and regeneration practices, and solar and renewable energy technologies are all worthy of public funding support. But the capacity of governments to develop and implement such support programs is seriously limited by WTO rules. These can be found in the WTO Agreement on Subsidies and Countervailing Duties, which prohibits the use of subsidies and delineates the responses that countries can take to counter the effects of subsidies, such as imposing countervailing duties on subsidized imports.

In this regard, Canada is again at the centre of a landmark WTO dispute,[73] this time concerning the use of subsidies to support research and development in aerospace, a sector with significant orientation to export sales. Whatever our views about the wisdom of such programs, WTO rules have now been interpreted in a way that dramatically constrains the capacity of governments to support domestic economic development strategies.

Research and Development Funding Under the WTO

Much of the Canadian government's enthusiasm for globalization rests on the notion that Canada's future economic prosperity depends on its ability to produce high-tech products for international markets. In order to compete in global markets, Canada has invested heavily in promoting the development of high-tech industries in Canada, largely through "Technology Partnerships Canada." Through this program, the government invests hundreds of millions of dollars annually to support research and development in Canada, much of it to the benefit of the aerospace industry. Supported by this and other programs, the Canadian aerospace industry has become a key industrial sector: 400 companies employ 60,000 people and account for $9.4 billion in annual exports.[74]

The importance of this sector may explain why Canada took up the cause of Bombardier, a major recipient of Technology Partnership support, to challenge Brazil's export development program for regional aircraft. For Canada isn't the only country playing the subsidies game to support aircraft manufacturers. Convinced that Brazilian subsidies overstepped the mark, Canada invoked the WTO dispute resolution process to challenge that country's supports to Embrear, an airplane manufacturer whose products compete directly with Bombardier's Canadair Regional Jet.

However, its aggressive use of WTO dispute resolution backfired when Brazil answered Canada's complaint with one of its own, going after Industry Canada's cherished subsidies programs and Canadian export development assistance.

While the WTO ruled that Brazil was unfairly subsidizing Embrear, its victory came at too great a cost to be of use to the victor. For the WTO panel also concluded that the Technologies Partnership Fund and the Canada Account were in breach of WTO rules. The latter is perhaps best known for funding Candu Reactor sales to countries that couldn't—or weren't willing to—pay directly for them.

Nevertheless, Canada quickly proclaimed victory by focusing attention on the WTO ruling on Brazil's export development program. Canada's Industry Minister also insisted that Canada would still be able to fund research and development programs; but industry spokespersons are much less confident. The 350-page WTO decision casts a large shadow over government policy options and, in this instance, over the future of programs to foster research and development, no matter how worthy the endeavour.

While some comfort might be taken from the WTO's criticism of the Canada Account, given the way in which this program has been used, this WTO ruling might actually have the effect of shifting Canada's industrial support programs to endeavours that are even less attractive than Atomic Energy of Canada Ltd. This is because the only truly safe terrain upon which to situate industrial development programs under WTO rules is defence spending, which is sheltered under its national security provisions from the type of challenge used to undermine Canadian supports for non-military industrial development.

As noted, the other type of government subsidy that is exempt under NAFTA is for oil exploration and development. In other words, free trade has singled out for favourable treatment the two foremost examples of unsustainable industrial development: weapons and fossil fuels.

A Comprehensive Regime

To this point, we have considered how the free trade agenda has undermined the capacity of governments to use tariffs and subsidies to foster economic development and create employment within their domestic economies. We now turn to two other WTO agreements, concerning investment and services. Both have enormous implications for workers seeking stable employment and reasonable compensation. Neither has anything to do with trade, per se, but everything to do with the capacity of governments to regulate domestic economic activity.

That such matters have become subject to WTO disciplines is the result of two strategic corporate priorities. The first was to establish a single, comprehensive codification of the rules upon which globalization depends. Given that global corporations have often fully integrated production, services, and investment functions, from their perspective this is essential.

The second strategy was to ensure that governments would respect these constraints on their capacity to govern. This, as we have seen, was accomplished by authorizing the use of trade sanctions to assure their compliance. Moreover, the WTO allows government to "cross retaliate" by imposing trade sanctions against those sectors where they will be most keenly felt. As we have seen in relating the case of the WTO challenge to Canadian cultural policies (see Chapter 4), countervailing duties can, for example, be applied to Canada's steel exports to compensate for purported losses to an unrelated services industry, magazine publishing. Thus, WTO trade sanctions can now be used to punish governments for initiatives that have nothing to do with trade.

The WTO Services Agreement—The MAI by Any Other Name

The Agreement on Trade in Services (the GATS) has far-reaching implications for employment in both the public and private sectors. We begin be considering its impacts on public services, an area where governments can play a direct role in job creation. The popular wisdom that governments have little to do with job creation and job growth ignores the critical role they play in creating the conditions—infrastructure, training, partnerships, subsidies—in which job creation and growth can occur. Such glib dismissals of government initiative also ignore the public sector employment associated with the delivery of services, from public utilities such as electricity, water, and waste, to health care and education. In Canada, these last two service areas are particularly important because of Canada's commitment to universality.

Thus, when governments say they are powerless to deal with problems such as chronic unemployment and growing underemployment, they are hoping we will overlook the fact that massive spending cuts for public services are adding significantly to the unemployment rate. Their attempts to deflect attention from their own culpability is understandable; but their readiness to declare their impotence is motivated by more than a desire to avoid the political consequences of abandoning Canadian workers. It is often also rooted in their ideological support for the free trade/privatization agenda: if health care, education, and other government services can be delivered by the private sector, then they should be.

At present, however, government programs and regulations constrain corporate access to the potentially lucrative provision of many services. In other instances, public sector monopolies provide education, health care, and many public utility services. Not surprisingly, corporations have seized on trade agreements as a means to tear down these barriers to the potential business opportunities these public service sectors represent.

This explains U.S. ambitions to enlarge the scope and application of the GATS. At present, most GATS disciplines apply only to services that governments volunteer for coverage under the Agreement. But the U.S. has now declared its ambition to make these obligations mandatory and has explicitly referred to the need to extend GATS to cover health and education services.[75] If it succeeds, we will see the current gradual erosion of support for public health care, education, and various utilities become a landslide of privatization.

Any doubt about the strategic importance of the GATS agreement is quickly resolved by a visit the WTO web site, which boastfully describes it as follows:

The GATS is the first multilateral agreement to provide legally enforceable rights to trade in all services. It has a built-in commitment to continuous liberalization through periodic negotiations. And **it is the world's first multilateral agreement on investment**, since it covers not just cross-border trade but every possible means of supplying a service, including the right to set up a commercial presence in the export market.

This description makes it apparent that, having failed to import a multilateral agreement on investment into the WTO by way of the OECD,[76] the U.S., on behalf of its corporate clients, has seized on the GATS as another way to achieve MAI objectives.

The extension of GATS disciplines concerning National Treatment to public sector services will transform Canadian health, education, and other public services into the U.S. private service delivery model. It would be difficult to overstate the impacts of this transformation on workers, as well as on the social fabric of this country. But it isn't only employment in the public sector that will be affected, because if the GATS is expanded, private sector jobs will also be at stake.

Service sector employment is the most rapidly expanding sector of the North American economy, and represents the one area in which the U.S. has a substantial balance of trade surplus. Thus the GATS has significant implications for telecommunications, finance, transportation, and many other service industries that are predominantly in the private sector. The potential impact of the GATS on industrial and manufacturing jobs came to light in a recent WTO dispute between Japan and Canada, concerning the Auto Pact.

Japan Challenges the Auto Pact

Japanese car manufacturers have long chafed at the constraints on their access to North American markets. Among other complaints, Japan has repeatedly claimed that the Auto Pact unfairly discriminates against its auto-makers. Under the Auto Pact, Canada maintains a 6.7% tariff on the importation of finished autos. To qualify for membership, companies must produce one car in Canada for every car they sell here.

Japan claims that in some cases it meets Auto Pact performance requirements and should be accorded duty-free access to Canadian markets. Canada disagrees. A study by the Canadian Auto Workers found that, under the Auto Pact, the Big Three auto-makers have committed six times as much investment as Japanese car producers have. In addition, compared to Japanese car producers, the Big Three account for 15 times the number of jobs in major auto plants and about 30 times the jobs in the supplier industries.

Japan, however, has pursued its claim by invoking WTO dispute procedures, citing concerns arising under several WTO Agreements, including the GATS. According to a trade journal account of Japan's reasons for invoking the GATS in support of its claim, it did so because "the import of autos involves transactions and distribution, which are services," and that imports of certain vehicles were handled by their service divisions.[77] Thus, Japan argued, differential import tariffs represented discrimination in services, and therefore a violation of Article II (Most Favoured Nation Treatment) obligations, under the GATS.

Japan's decision to invoke the GATS agreement in support of its challenge to the Auto Pact reveals just how far-reaching implications of this services agreement may be for all sectors of the economy, even those that would not traditionally be considered part of the service sector.

Japan's use of the GATS to mount an argument against tariffs on manufactured products is also illustrative of the redundancy built into many WTO and NAFTA agreements. Thus, when nations invoke WTO dispute resolution processes to challenge another government's policies, laws, or programs, they invariably use a shotgun approach, alleging violations of several WTO rules or agreements. Moreover, dispute resolution panels consistently respond by finding several grounds upon which to impugn the government initiative under attack.

Finally, on the subject of services, it is important to stress that, while a services agreement is housed within NAFTA, Canada has not formally acceded to its wholesale application to health care, education, and other service sectors. It is critical, then, that determined efforts be made to resist the expansion of the framework currently in place in the GATS agreement. In this, the capacity of civil society to frustrate the progress of the globalization agenda has never been stronger.

As noted, the other WTO agreement critical to jobs and wages is the WTO Agreement on Trade-Related Investment Measures (the TRIMS Agreement). Because of the enormity of their implications, we have dedicated an entire chapter to international investment agreements such as the one entrenched in Chapter 11 of NAFTA, and that proposed as the Multilateral Agreement on Investment (MAI) which is now being revived to put real teeth in the WTO TRIMs Agreement.

Protecting Workers' Rights in the WTO?

How has organized labour responded to the daunting challenges of free trade? In many ways, the labour movement in Canada has been in the forefront of efforts to resist the free trade agenda. In fact, the response of Canadian labour has been far more determined and collaborative than is the case for U.S. and European labour groups. However, the advent of these regimes has confronted the trade union movement with a dilemma. Should it continue to take an uncompromising position against a global corporate agenda that is in many ways firmly established? Should it attempt to find some compromise that would build into this new global regime some protection for the fundamental rights of working people? Or can it do both at the same time?

While some trade unions have maintained an uncompromising opposition to globalization, several labour federations have decided upon a course of constructive engagement and have advocated the inclusion of a "Workers' Rights Clause" in international trade agreements. Perhaps the most prominent of these proposals is the one being advanced by the International Confederation of Free Trade Unions (ICFTU), which proposes:

> The contracting parties agree to take steps to ensure the observance of the minimum labour standards specified by an advisory committee to be established by the WTO and the ILO [the International Labour Organization], and including those of freedom of association and right to collective bargaining, the minimum age of employment, discrimination, equal remuneration, and forced labour.

The ILO is a tripartite organization comprising representatives of government, labour, and business; it is affiliated with the UN and has a mandate to define and monitor international labour standards. The fundamental rights referred to in the ICFTU proposals more or less replicate those covered by seven core ILO conventions and include the right to form free trade unions independent of state interference, and the right to free collective bargaining, equality of employment, and freedom from forced labour and child labour. Unfortunately, many of these basic labour rights are routinely violated by many countries, including those which have formally ratified these conventions or proclaimed their support for them. The absence of any meaningful enforcement mechanism explains why these ILO rules are honoured more in the breach than in the observance.

To address the need for credible sanctions, the ICFTU proposes a fairly elaborate monitoring and compliance regime. Non-compliance might ultimately result in the suspension of a nation's privileges under the WTO. In this regard it is important to contrast these proposals with the NAFTA labour side-agreement, which Canadian labour groups, unlike many of their U.S. counterparts, were adamant in rejecting as a reasonable trade-off for the enormous gains that NAFTA created for the corporate agenda. Today, no one could credibly argue that this NAFTA side-deal has improved conditions for working people in any NAFTA country.[78] Unlike the NAFTA side-agreement, ICFTU proposals would require adherence to ILO defined rights on pain of trade sanction.

The accompanying box describes some of the impacts that free trade has had on Canadian workers since the advent of this regime a decade ago, and its extension in NAFTA five years later. For, notwithstanding the labour side-agreement, NAFTA has been a disaster for millions of workers in NAFTA countries, and has done nothing to further the interests of tens of millions more.[79] If corporations and trade officials succeed in establishing at the WTO the tariff, services, and investment rules currently in NAFTA, Canadian workers should brace themselves for another round of corporate restructuring not unlike the one that produced such disastrous results over the past decade.

Between 1989 and 1993, Ontario reported 452 major manufacturing facility closures, (half were foreign-owned—mainly U.S.—companies) and 65% of these closures were permanent.

A 1992 *Wall Street Journal* survey of 455 senior corporate executives indicated that 25% of them planned to use NAFTA to bargain down wages; and 40% were planning to move some production facilities to Mexico.

A 1996 study of 500 union organizing drives indicated that 62% of employers threatened to close or move their operations rather than negotiate with a union.

Economic integration in North America has cost manufacturing jobs in all three countries, but Canada has been worst hit. It experienced a contraction of 255,000 jobs, 12.8% during 1988–96. This is three times the proportionate U.S. decline.

The percentage of workers employed part-time has grown in all three countries. Increases are largest in Canada, where part-timers now comprise 18.6% of the employed work force. In 1994, temporary workers comprised 9.0% of the Canadian work force, nearly three times their proportional presence a decade earlier.

Even with shifts to much less secure employment and more poorly-paying jobs, Canada's official employment rate is the highest of any decade since WW2.

Or would a meaningful labour rights clause in the WTO produce a different result? To answer this question, it is first important to recognize that there are key differences between NAFTA and the WTO when it comes to tariff elimination, services, and investment rules. Under the WTO, governments retain some important tools for developing domestic economic strategies attuned to the interests of working people. These options are no longer available to Canada because of NAFTA constraints. Therefore, the first priority for labour should be to resist extension to the WTO of the corporate beachhead established in NAFTA. Given the pervasive and pernicious impacts of these aspects of the globalization agenda, a labour rights clause should not be seen as a reasonable compromise for the further reduction of tariff powers, or for the establishment of substantive WTO agreements on investments and services.

However, if the further expansion of the WTO is stopped, there would still be limits to the efficacy of a labour rights clause. For there are fundamental contradictions between the interests of workers, on the one hand, and those of deregulation, privatization, and free trade, on the other. Indeed, the free trade agenda is directly opposed to worker rights insofar as it espouses the unfettered growth of corporate revenues and profits. Workers' wages, taxes to support infrastructure, environmental and conservation laws, and public service monopolies all present impediments to these corporate imperatives.

It isn't as if workers, the environment, and social services are unintended casualties of globalization; they are rather the inevitable *targets* of a global model that often regards these interests as detrimental to corporate growth and profitability. Therefore, as we have seen, the goal of free trade policies is to establish a comprehensive regime intended to contain, or even eliminate, the capacity of governments to regulate corporate activity for the purpose of achieving labour, environmental, or other societal goals. It is fair to say that there are no provisions of NAFTA or WTO agreements that are not intended to serve this corporate agenda: they are uniform in their purpose.

This should, accordingly, raise serious questions about the potential effectiveness of grafting onto such agreements a clause that cuts so thoroughly against the grain of the most fundamental objectives of these trade regimes. It isn't whether workers' rights are worthy of protection through international agreements, or whether trade measures should be used to force corporations to respect these rights—the answer to both questions is clearly yes. Rather, the question is whether these goals can be accomplished by attaching the means of achieving them to trade regimes created to defeat the very goals a "labour rights clause" would promote.

But, if WTO rules are going to be with us for some time to come, isn't it irresponsible to ignore opportunities to ameliorate the worst effects of this regime? In response to this challenge, the Canadian Labour Congress has refined ICFTU proposals in an effort to counter the unleavened impacts of free trade on workers in both the North and South. In doing so, it has also expressed pointed criticism of the one-sided nature of the trade liberalization agenda that has been entrenched by NAFTA and the WTO. It has called upon the federal government to reject any further liberalization initiatives "until a strong social and environmental framework is put in place," which it argues should be "the central focus of the coming WTO round."[80] As to the substance of that social and environmental framework, the CLC has put forward several proposals. The most pivotal is the suggestion that

> Canada support the establishment of a joint WTO–ILO Working Party on a workers' rights clause, and support the insertion of a clause in the WTO. Any country found to be in violation would be so advised, and technical and other support would be made available to bring about compliance over a reasonable period of time. In the final instance, WTO sanctions would apply, as in other cases of extended non-compliance with a WTO ruling.

Recognizing the entrenched biases of the WTO, the CLC proposes the establishment of a joint WTO–ILO committee to monitor government compliance and investigate alleged violations. A country found in breach of its obligations to respect core labour rights would be offered "technical and other support," but would ultimately face trade sanctions should non-compliance persist. By putting meaningful enforcement mechanisms at the disposal of the ILO, the CLC proposal also seeks to address the long-standing problem of chronic non-compliance with ILO conventions.

In putting forward these proposals, the CLC has recognized that they will not do a great deal to reduce the downward pressure that globalization is exerting on wages in developed countries. Indeed the existence of fully developed labour rights in Canada did little to lessen the impacts of free trade with the U.S. and then Mexico. While NAFTA did nothing to directly dismantle worker rights, it did profoundly undermine the bargaining clout that unions could bring to the table. Because free trade meant that companies could move to low-wage jurisdictions and still have secured access to Canada's markets and resources, Canadian labour was suddenly forced to compete with workers willing to accept wages that were a fraction of those paid in Canada.

Rather, the CLC foresees workers in developing countries to be the principal beneficiaries of such rights. It argues that a labour clause would "equalize conditions among developing countries at similar stages of development" by gradually raising incomes and improving working conditions. Such rights would be of particular value to workers in the most repressive regimes. The CLC also points to evidence that links respect for core labour rights with faster growth. "Higher incomes in developing countries would also modestly lessen downward pressure on wages in developed countries, expanding the markets available for developing countries."

Appreciating that a labour rights clause could only play a small part in answering the growing problems of the global economy, the CLC advocates the inclusion of a such a clause to provide some counterbalance to what would otherwise be the unadulterated downward pressures on wages, living standards and social conditions that free trade rules exert. Whether this strategy proves to be effective or not, it will be critical for labour movements to direct the lion's share of their resources toward preventing the expansion of the WTO, and toward dismantling many elements of the deregulatory framework already entrenched in the WTO and NAFTA.

We need trade agreements that discipline capital and corporations, not trade agreements that prevent governments from doing so. Admittedly, this is an ambitious agenda, but any objective assessment of the globalization paradigm leads to the inescapable conclusion that it is simply unsustainable. The question is not whether it will collapse under the weight of its own rapacious appetites—that is inevitable; it is rather whether we can transform this system in time to avert the catastrophic damage to workers, ecosystems, and human society that globalization has already begun.

10

Patents, Biopiracy, and Intellectual Property Rights

In legal terms, property ownership can be described as the right to exclude others from use or enjoyment. Many countries have established domestic regimes for creating intellectual property by way of patents, trademarks, or copyright. Accordingly, intellectual property rights (IPRs) allow authors, inventors, and others to monopolize the fruits of their creative efforts. In granting these rights of exclusive ownership, society seeks to reward invention in order to foster further innovation. By denying others the right to take immediate advantage of new products, technologies or ideas, society is seeking to create a balance with the rights of innovators that will ultimately serve societal goals by assuring the continued flow of new products and processes from which all will benefit.

Historically, the extent to which intellectual property rights were recognized and protected was considered to be entirely the prerogative of domestic policy. Seeking to establish the appropriate balance between the rights of innovators and of other citizens was considered best left to those who could judge the particular and often unique needs of their communities.

With the advent of globalization and the introduction of technologies (e.g., VCRs and drug manufacturing techniques) that allowed intellectual products to be easily copied or reproduced, the originators of those products (and in particular U.S.-based pharmaceutical and media corporations) began to exert pressure on other governments to adopt U.S.-style patent protection laws. A principal device for exerting that pressure was the threat of unilateral trade sanctions against governments that were seen to be turning a blind eye to the "unauthorized" use of intellectual products within their jurisdiction.

The next logical step, of course, was to establish an intellectual property-rights regime in GATT, where it would benefit from the powerful compliance mechanisms contained in trade agreements.

Thus these same corporations spearheaded an international campaign that culminated with the inclusion of the Agreement on Trade-Related Aspects of Intellectual Property Rights [TRIPs] as part of the WTO. In the simplest terms, the TRIPs Agreement requires all WTO parties to adopt, as their own domestic law, a system of intellectual property rights protection based on the U.S. model.

Accordingly, the TRIPs Agreement sets out comprehensive rules for copyright, trademark, and patent protection. Of these intellectual property rights, patent protection is arguably the most important from a broad societal perspective. Patent rights, for example, apply to virtually all technological innovation including medicinal drugs, environmentally sound technologies, and many forms of biotechnology. As we will see, the implementation of this global patent-protection regime is already having an enormous impact on our ability to achieve such diverse goals as protecting biodiversity or containing spiralling drug costs.

TRIPs vs. Free Trade

There are several serious problems associated with imposing a U.S.-style intellectual property-rights regime as the international standard. However, before examining the impacts that this new trade regime is likely to have, there are two general observations that are worth making.

The first is that the essential thrust of the TRIPs Agreement stands in stark contrast with the ideology of free markets and deregulated trade. Where virtually every other aspect of the WTO regime seeks to limit the regulatory prerogatives of governments, this regime imposes a positive obligation to legislate, and to do so in very precise terms. This is strong evidence that, while the ideology of free trade is important, it is at its root little more than a rationale for the growth and profit maximization imperatives of large corporations. When these corporate interests conflict with the ideology of unregulated markets, the latter will give way.

Under the IPR Rules of the WTO

All countries must establish domestic IPR legislation, as well as the administrative and judicial mechanisms that are necessary to give them effect.

Patent rights must be made available for any invention, whether products or processes, in all fields of technology provided that they are new, involve an inventive step, and are capable of industrial application.

Patent rights must also be made available for micro-organisms and for the protection of plant varieties; however, plants and animals may be excluded from these patent regimes.

The minimum period of patent protection is to be 20 years.

Various judicial and border inspection rights must exist to allow patent holders the effective means to enforce their IPRs.

The second noteworthy aspect of the TRIPs Agreement is that, notwithstanding the qualification that it is about "trade-related" IPRs, the provisions of this agreement apply to all products and processes, whether they are traded or not. In fact, in very large measure, this "trade agreement" will apply to goods that are entirely produced and consumed locally. In this way the TRIPs Agreement extends the reach of international trade rules directly into a critical sphere of domestic policy and law. In doing so, it represents an unprecedented incursion into the sovereign authority of nation-states to determine the conduct of affairs within their national borders.

It is beyond the scope of this guide to delve into all aspects of the TRIPs Agreement. Rather, this chapter focuses on one particularly problematic dimension of the TRIPs regime: the rules concerning patent rights.

Biodiversity, Farmers' Rights, and Intellectual Property

Under the provisions of the TRIPs Agreement, governments may exclude various inventions from patentability. These include "plants and animals other than micro-organisms, and essentially biological processes for the production of plants and animals other than non-biological and microbiological processes." But countries must provide "patent protection for plant varieties, either by patents or by an effective *sui generis* (of their own kind) system."[81]

The New Frontier

Because traditional or indigenous knowledge is not recognized as intellectual property, and because the collective innovation of generations of farmers is similarly alien to the technological and industrial model inherent in modern patent law, multinational corporations feel free to appropriate global genetic resources without any recognition of the rights of communal but non-proprietary ownership. In important ways, this exploitation of the genetic frontier parallels the process of colonization and conquest of the Americas that similarly disregarded the collective or communal character of "ownership" in cultures that have not defined the world entirely in terms of proprietary interests.

The likely impact of these provisions on biodiversity and Third World agricultural production has raised considerable concern. In fact, several non-governmental organizations have assailed these rules as authorizing the wholesale piracy of genetic resources from developing countries and the appropriation, without compensation, of traditional and indigenous knowledge. Thus, Southern NGOs point to the practices of certain pharmaceutical and agri-corporations that have taken out patents on products and processes derived from genetic resources they have simply appropriated from developing countries. Having thus acquired a global mandate to monopolize the use of these "innovations," those same corporations can then enforce their new proprietary rights even in those countries from which the genetic resources were originally taken.

It is also apparent that, in practice, the innovation for which patent protection is acquired is often the product of very modest investment or effort. For example, a U.S.-based corporation has been granted a process patent for extracting the active ingredient of the Neem tree that has provided a source of medicine and other products to indigenous cultures for millennia.[82] It is unlikely that the process it has patented represents any significant innovation of indigenous extractive techniques, but, by virtue of having acquired this patent, and because of the TRIPs Agreement, this corporation can acquire a global monopoly that can be worth truly astronomical sums during the 20 years for which protection is guaranteed.

If the policy rationale for patent protection is creating some balance between the interests of society and those of inventors, that balance would appear to be wildly out of kilter in many of the cases where patents have been issued.

Another area of concern relates to the adverse effects these rules will have on the diversity of cultivated crops and on farmers in the developing countries. Because informal innovation is not accorded any protection, the genetically diverse resources of wild germ-plasm or "land races" are excluded from the proprietary regimes of the TRIPs Agreement. Not only does this mean that these resources can be appropriated without compensation, but it also means that no financial incentive exists to conserve these resources.[83] This is just one factor, but nevertheless an important one in spurring the abandonment of traditional plants in favour of hybrid and genetically modified varieties that are very much part of the high-yield—and even higher-input—model of modern agricultural production.

While all aspects of the WTO are amenable to further negotiation and amendment, the potential enormity of the impacts associated with these types of patents were considered sufficient to warrant mandatory review.

Technology Transfer

The need to ensure the transfer of environmentally sound technology [EST] is a particularly important priority for the goals of sustainable development. That is why, for example, the Montreal Protocol, the Biodiversity Convention, and the Climate Change Convention all include provisions that make technology transfer a critical element of the strategies those agreements establish.[84] It is easy, then, to see how the provisions of the TRIPs Agreement would interfere with this objective, because by its very intent it seeks to constrain the availability, and increase the cost, of using new products and innovations that might, for example, provide better pollution prevention techniques, improve the efficiency of technology, or produce breakthroughs in solar energy or photovoltaics.

Thus, the TRIPs Agreement will likely slow the transfer of environmentally beneficial technologies to developing countries. However, there is one important way in which these adverse impacts can be ameliorated because of an important exception to IPR protection that can be found in Article 31 of the TRIPs Agreement. Under this rule, governments can license the use of patented products and processes without the consent of the patent holder for use either by government or by third parties (i.e., individuals and corporations).

In order to issue such compulsory licenses, governments must observe certain conditions. The most important of these is the obligation to ensure that the patent holder is "paid adequate remuneration

Mandatory Patent Licenses under Section 308 of the U.S. Clean Air Act

On occasion, a party attempting to comply with a standard of the Clean Air Act [CAA] may be unable to meet the standard without resorting to a patented technology. CAA Section 308 provides a mechanism by which such a non-complying party may obtain a patent license where it has been unsuccessful in obtaining a license on its own. Under CAA Section 308, the United States may require the owner of the patented technology to grant the non-complying party a patent license in exchange for a reasonable royalty, if the patented technology is necessary to meet the requirements in certain sections of the CAA.

The North American Free Trade Agreement (NAFTA) imposes certain limits on the ability of the United States to force patent owners to grant licenses under their patents [as does now the WTO TRIPs Agreement]. Therefore the EPA issued this rule to ensure that implementation of CAA Section 308 conformed with the requirements of NAFTA Article 1709(10) [WTO TRIPs Article 31]. The rule established the policies and procedures that the EPA would follow prior to applying to the Attorney General for a mandatory license under a patent covering a technology necessary to enable compliance with the new stationary sources standards, hazardous air pollutants standards, or motor vehicle emission standards of the CAA. [Environmental Protection Agency 40 CFR Part 95, [FRL-5131-5]

in the circumstances of each case, taking into account the economic value of the authorization." In other words, royalties.

In fact, just such a compulsory licensing regime has been established under the U.S. Clean Air Act, which is described in the preceding box.

The TRIPs Agreement as a Prototype

Finally, perhaps the most noteworthy aspect of the TRIPs agreement has to do with what it reveals about the extent to which a trade regime can be used to accomplish key policy objectives. Imagine if environmental goals, for example, were taken as seriously as patent rights. If one looks at the TRIPs Agreement as a model for international agreements to protect biodiversity, or for confronting climate change, it is easier to appreciate the enormous potential that trade agreements have for securing environmental and other societal goals—if only they were written for that purpose.

For example, if the WTO were transformed into an organization that was as concerned about the impacts of climate change as it is currently preoccupied with the growth of transnational pharmaceutical companies, then we would have an Agreement on Trade-Related

Measures to Combat Global Warming. Such an agreement would require all WTO members to:

- adopt domestic laws (which would be delineated with some specificity) to stabilize greenhouse-gas emissions at 1990 levels;

- provide for customs inspection, seizure, and even the disposal of goods that were produced in ways that violate the provisions of the Agreement;

- establish administrative civil remedies and criminal sanctions for any breach of the legislation or regulations mandated by the Agreement; and

- authorize the use of trade sanctions, including cross-retaliatory measures such as prohibiting the export of energy or energy products, against any jurisdiction that was in breach of its obligations under the Agreement.

If these provisions seem rather ambitious, it is important to recognize that each merely translates the actual requirements and rights that have been established by the TRIPs Agreement into terms that are relevant to confronting climate change. It is a measure of how much work is ahead of us that a proposal to treat the goal of addressing climate change as seriously as pharmaceutical patents would no doubt be greeted with complete incredulity by the WTO.

It is important then that governments be encouraged to explain why they consider patent protection a much higher priority than global warming, health care, biodiversity loss, or any number of other pressing ecological and social problems.

A Citizen's Agenda

It is very likely that the compulsory licensing provisions of the TRIPs Agreement will be tested as governments take advantage of the opportunity to issue such licenses, and the assessment of what represents "adequate compensation" in this context will largely determine the extent to which the IPR rules interfere with technology transfer objectives.

For these reasons, it will be important for civil society to insist that governments establish compulsory licensing rules to aid technology transfer, and to support a liberal interpretation of this exception to the monopoly protections accorded under the TRIPs agreement. Moreover, compulsory licensing rules should also become the subject of protocols to multilateral environment agreements (MEAs) that include technology transfer provisions.

However, in the context of Parliamentary committee hearings on Canadian drug patent protection legislation, the government has taken the position that NAFTA and the WTO preclude the adoption of compulsory licensing regimes, such as the one maintained by the U.S. EPA. Yet many other countries have and maintain compulsory licensing systems for patent medicines.[85] The protests of powerlessness by Canada's federal government provided an unfortunate example of how imaginary trade constraints can serve as a smokescreen for politicians to hide behind.

Developing literacy in trade matters seems to be the only sure way to know whether governments are bluffing or not when they claim their hands are tied by WTO rules. The provisions of the TRIPs Agreement are not particularly lengthy or complex, but the government is betting that no one will make the effort to see whether its claims of powerlessness are justified.

Trade-Related Investment Measures

The Agreement on Trade-Related Investment Measures (TRIMs) provides only a rudimentary framework for the investor rights that the International Chamber of Commerce and others were hoping to entrench in the WTO. Their failure to achieve this goal is in large measure explained by the determined resistance of developing nations that stayed united in their opposition to the investor rights agenda.

Having being turned aside at the WTO, the sponsors of an international treaty for investment protection lost no time in recasting their project as a Multilateral Agreement on Investment (MAI) and went in search of more sympathic venues. This they thought they had found in the Organization for Economic Cooperation and Development (OECD), a club for the world's most developed nations.

But when France withdrew from MAI negotiations in October 1998, efforts to establish a global investment regime under the auspices of the OECD were effectively scuttled. Now, once again, there is talk of moving the MAI initiative back into the WTO. Moreover, the prototype for the MAI is alive and well and can be found in

Chapter 11 of NAFTA, where it currently serves as an important weapon for attacking government measures for achieving public health, environmental protection, and other societal goals. Similar investor protections can also be found in dozens of bilateral investment agreements that have very quietly been negotiated over the past few years. For example, without any public discussion or debate, Canada negotiated over two dozen foreign investment treaties with countries from Eastern Europe, South America and the Caribbean during the past decade. For these reasons the investor-rights agenda is as relevant today as it was before the wheels recently came off the OECD-MAI cart.

In the simplest terms, international investment treaties create a broadly-defined list of investor rights to conduct business free from government oversight or regulatory control. This is accomplished by explicitly prohibiting an extensive catalogue of government policies, laws, and programs. To guarantee that governments respect these new limits on their authority, these treaties also include very powerful and secretive legal enforcement mechanisms that can be invoked by any foreign investor.

While the investor rights agenda is constructed on the same platform of National Treatment and Most Favoured Nation Treatment that is common to all WTO Agreements, it goes much further in two critical ways. The first is to allow individual investors virtually unqualified access to international enforcement mechanisms that may be invoked by them directly against nation-states.

It would be difficult to overstate the implications of this radical departure from the norms of international treaty law which, with the exception of international human rights, has never created enforceable rights to the benefit of individuals, let alone transnational corporations. In other words, under NAFTA and MAI prototypes, for the purposes of enforcement, foreign investors are accorded the same status as nation-states.

The other critical departure of this proposed investment regime from the norms of international trade law is to be found under the heading Performance Requirements, which actually constrains the implementation of domestic investment regulation even when applied only to domestic investors. Thus, under the rubric of negotiating an international treaty, governments would abandon their prerogatives to regulate investment even in the most local context.

The following assessment considers these and other key elements of the agenda to establish a global investor-rights agreement in more detail, but first addresses the highly secretive way in which this agenda has been pursued.

The "Stealth Agreement"

There can be little doubt that it has been a deliberate strategy of those negotiating international investment agreements to limit public awareness of and debate about such treaties. MAI negotiations, for example, proceeded entirely behind closed doors and were to have been concluded well in advance of being made public. The approach appears based on the well-founded assumption that the MAI would not survive the light of public scrutiny. In fact, negotiations were such a closely-guarded secret that, even within governments, few ministers and hardly any backbenchers were aware of its progress or significance. Some members of the federal Liberal government have even denounced the MAI as a "stealth agreement."[86]

Fortunately, a leaked copy of the text became available just before negotiations were originally to have been concluded. Ever since, protests have mounted as the profound dimensions of this investment treaty became known to citizens in Canada and other OECD countries. In addition to opposition from public interest and labour groups, even some governments are now voicing their concerns about the MAI process.

The following analysis should shed light on why this proposed investment treaty has prompted such determined and widespread opposition. While NAFTA's Investment Chapter represents the real-life example of the type of investment protections that are being promoted for the TRIMs Agreement of the WTO, the MAI is probably a better guide to this agenda, since it has already been revived as part of pending WTO negotiations. This distinction is important because in several ways the MAI built upon and would extend the investor rights enshrined in NAFTA and many bilateral treaties.

International Investor-Rights Agreements in Five Easy Pieces

1. Who Is a Foreign Investor?

It is clear that the investors who benefit from the protections established by these investment treaties will, in almost all cases, be corporations, and that "protection" for them means the freedom to operate without being subject to government regulation. It is also important to note that, under present proposals, "investment" would be defined very broadly to include every kind of asset owned or controlled, directly or indirectly, by an investor— including any type of business, rights under contract, and even intellectual property.

Particularly important from an environmental point of view is that, unlike NAFTA, proposals to expand WTO investment rules would define investment to include rights arising by way of concessions, licenses, authorizations, and permits. This definition removes any doubt that fishing, mining, energy, or forest licenses—or any other permit to exploit public natural resources—would give rise to enforceable investor rights.[87] Because the central reference point of any investment treaty is the way in which it defines "investment," the broader this definition the greater the scope and application of the entire agreement.

While international investor rights are predominantly created in favour of foreign investors, the Performance Requirement rules of these treaties apply equally to domestic investors. This is one of the more astonishing features of these agreements because, as we will discuss below, under such international treaties Canada is actually abandoning its domestic legislative prerogatives to regulate all investors, including Canadian investors, operating entirely within Canada.

Giving Foreign Investors Preferential Treatment

One aspect of these international investment treaties that has drawn particular criticism from all sectors is the preferential treatment it accords foreign investors.[88] Thus, and as we have noted, prohibitions against government regulations in the form of Performance Requirements treat domestic and foreign investors in the same way. Many other aspects of these treaties do not. This is true under NAFTA, as well.[89] Thus NAFTA establishes an array of new investor rights that are only available to foreign companies and individuals, thus reducing Canadian citizens and companies to the status of second-class citizens in their own country.

2. National Treatment: All of the Rights, None of the Responsibility

The first principle of NAFTA and its progeny is the extension of National Treatment to foreign investors. By doing so, international investment treaties dramatically extend the reach of trade disciplines to many spheres of domestic economic policy by prohibiting government actions that favour domestic companies or investors. Thus, foreign investors and corporations must be given every right, concession, or privilege that a government might extend to local companies or communities. When these rules are considered against the objectives of many domestic resource management policies, several conflicts become readily apparent.

Take British Columbia, for example. Like many other jurisdictions, the essential goal of B.C. forest policy is to optimize the value of public resources to the benefit of the province, its communities, and its residents. Section 2 of the Forest Renewal Act of B.C. puts it this way:

> The purpose of this Act is to renew the forest economy of British Columbia, enhance the productive capacity and environmental value of forest lands, create jobs, provide training for forest workers, and strengthen communities.

Indeed, these are the common themes of several other provincial laws and programs. The same priority access to Crown resources can also be found in federal fishery policy and law. For example, priority access to Crown fishery resources is explicitly accorded Canadians and First Nations under Canada's Coastal Fisheries Protection Act, the Fisheries Act, and several federal-provincial agreements such as the Agreement on the Management of the Pacific Salmon Fishery.

By definition, however, measures that favour Canadian citizens, companies, and communities discriminate against foreign citizens and enterprises. In other words, they represent precisely the type of discriminatory treatment that these investment treaties were drafted to eliminate. It is this fundamental contradiction that explains why so many aspects of Canadian natural resources law and regulation are incompatible with the rules of the MAI and NAFTA.

In the context of investor rights, National Treatment would, for example, prohibit:

- policies that favour community land tenure or resource management rights,

- citizenship requirements for those seeking fishing or woodlot licenses, and

- subsidies to support community economic development such as are provided by forest or Fisheries Renewal B.C.

Another area in which unconstrained foreign access is incompatible with provincial policy and law concerns access to Canadian water resources.

The Special Case of Water

Canada has one of the most abundant supplies of fresh water in the world, but most of our water flows northward far from our major population centres. And where our population is located, in a narrow ribbon along the U.S. boarder, our water supplies are becoming increasingly polluted. While there have been many proposals to divert northern water to southern consumers, the enormous environmental implications of such projects have given rise to determined opposition by environmental groups and others who have managed to thwart such proposals.

Nevertheless, many entrepreneurs and some politicians continue their attempts to turn this critical public resource into private profits. That is why, ever since the advent of free trade, Canadians have worried that trade rules would one day be used to challenge Canadian efforts to restrict bulk water exports. They needn't hold their breath any longer, because a U.S.-based company, Sun Belt Water Inc., has decided to do just that.

The Sun Belt claim follows the lead of the other U.S. corporations (Ethyl Corporation and S.D. Myers) which have taken advantage of the powerful enforcement provisions in NAFTA's investment chapter to challenge other Canadian environmental laws. Relying on these rules, Sun Belt is seeking more than US$200 million from Canada because of B.C. legislation banning bulk water exports. The company claims that B.C.'s law violates several NAFTA-based investor rights including, in this case, its right to export B.C. water by tanker to California.

Sun Belt argues that it is entitled to the same access to Canadian water that Canadians enjoy. Anything less is discriminatory and offends the principle of National Treatment, a cornerstone of free trade. Having been denied that access by B.C.'s export ban, it now claims compensation for the profits it would have made had free trade rules been observed.

For years, the federal government has assured Canadians that water would not be subject to the type of claim that Sun Belt has just made. There is only one certain way for Canada to guarantee that protection and that is to negotiate within NAFTA a clear and unequivocal exception for water. More importantly, Canada, the U.S., and Mexico should also rectify another serious error that was made during NAFTA negotiations, which was to allow foreign corporations direct access to NAFTA's powerful enforcement machinery.

The "Tragedy of the Commons" and Your Community

The principle of providing foreign corporations precisely the same access to Crown resources as is available to Canadian citizens, companies and First Nations offends many people's sense of fairness or equity. It is also clearly incompatible with any notion of First Nation entitlements or land claims. However, there is also a strong environmental rationale for "discriminating" in favour of local communities and First Nations when it comes to allocating public natural resources.

When access to resources entails no obligation of stewardship, the result has inevitably spelled disaster. Sometimes referred to as the "tragedy of the commons," these are the dynamics that underlie the current crises affecting global ecosystems, from our oceans to the Earth's atmosphere. Because of the absence of any meaningful international controls, the exploitation of these global or common resources is effectively unregulated or supervised.

In this context, there is little incentive for any particular user to practise conservation or restraint. Moreover, the logic of "if I don't, someone else will" is reinforced by the dictates of global competitiveness that punish any corporation that defers immediate profits in favour of longer-term or more sustainable returns. This has unleashed rapacious rates of resource consumption that soon exhaust non-renewable resources or overwhelm the capacity of renewable resources to regenerate.

By imposing international market imperatives, while reducing local government control, the investor-rights regimes effectively subject domestic natural resources to the same destructive dynamics that have devastated the global commons. In other words, natural resources that were once subject to national priorities and controls would now become the common property of all foreign and domestic investors. At the same time, the capacity of government to impose conservation constraints would be weakened, and in some instances explicitly removed. The result is certain to accelerate already unsustainable rates of resource exploitation.

The challenge before us is to find new ways to strengthen the role of local communities when it comes to natural resources management. Those that must live with the consequences of destructive resource practices will often have the greatest stake in ensuring long-term sustainable management. They should, therefore, be given a central role in determining local management issues and priorities. But, under NAFTA and like agreements, such preferential treatment would clearly offend the principle of National Treatment. ⁿ

3. Performance Requirements: Prohibiting Government Regulation

Under the heading Performance Requirements, NAFTA and other international investment treaties set out extensive and broadly defined lists of prohibited government policies, laws, and programs. Moreover, as we have noted, the application of these constraints is much broader than for other provisions of these investment agreements because they apply to investors "of a Contracting Party or of a non-Contracting Party," i.e., to all investors, whatever their country of origin.

In other words, under the rubric of negotiating an international treaty, Canada has actually agreed not to regulate its own investors, or those from any other country, whether that country was a party to NAFTA or not.

Performance Requirements also go well beyond the principle of non-discrimination applied by National Treatment, because this rule prohibits government measures no matter how equitable or even-handed their application to foreign investors.

Finally, by providing that "a Contracting Party shall not impose, enforce or maintain any of the following requirements..." Performance Requirement constraints may actually apply retroactively to regulations and agreements that predate the Treaty.

Among the list of actions that are prohibited are government regulations that would require an investor to

- achieve a given level or percentage of domestic content, or to purchase goods or services locally;

- transfer environmentally sound technology;

- supply local markets or value-added producers;

- achieve a given level or value of production, investment, employment, or research and development; or

- hire local or even Canadian residents.

If we are to contain and ultimately rein in unsustainable resource management practices that are damaging once-abundant and diverse ecosystems, we must work together to build more diverse resource economies; promote local economic development; foster environmentally sound technologies; and ensure "just transitions" for workers. Unfortunately, NAFTA and proposed WTO investment rules will make each and every one of these goals far more difficult, if not impossible, to achieve. Ɲ

Community Economic Development and Sustainable Resource Management

For many decades, Canadian natural resources policies have sought to maximize the value added to raw natural resources before being exported. At times these policies have been expressed in the form of bans on the export of raw logs or unprocessed fish. In other instances, Canadian law has actually required investment in value-added processing as a condition for gaining access to Crown resources. For example, the following box contrasts the requirements of the Forest Act with certain performance requirements of the MAI. These contradictions are literally one example of dozens, if not hundreds, of similar conflicts that are revealed when Canadian laws are compared with MAI and NAFTA rules.

Forest Act Requirements

Section 127: Unless exempted, timber that is harvested from Crown land, in a tree-farm license area, and wood residue produced from the timber, must be:

a) used in British Columbia, or

b) manufactured in British Columbia into: (i) lumber, (ii) sawn wood products, other than lumber, manufactured to an extent required by the Minister.

Conflicting MAI Provisions

Performance Requirement sub-paragraph:

b) Parties shall not require investors to achieve a given level or percentage of domestic content;

> h) Parties shall not require investors to supply one or more of the goods it produces to a specific regions;
>
> j) Parties shall not require investors to hire a given level of nationals.

4. Expropriation: Private Property Rights in a Global Constitution

While National Treatment and Performance Requirements rules will undermine the economic, community development, and industrial policies needed to support truly sustainable resource management, the most direct assault on environmental law and policy can be found under the heading of Investment Protection:

> A Contracting Party shall not expropriate, or nationalize directly or indirectly, an investment in its territory of an investor of another Contracting Party, or take any measure or measures having equivalent effect, (hereinafter referred to as "expropriation") except accompanied by payment of prompt, adequate and effective compensation—equivalent to the fair market value of the expropriated investment.

It has long been the goal of property rights advocates to have these private rights entrenched in Canada's constitution. Their campaign is primarily directed at Canadian laws that assert that private property rights must give way, in certain instances, to the greater public good. Thus, challenges to such measures as zoning bylaws or habitat protection laws on the grounds that they interfere with private property rights have been consistently rebuffed by Canadian courts. But what has been unacceptable to the courts, and rejected as part of Canadian constitutional reform, now appears to have been accomplished by NAFTA and would be expanded under an MAI-type treaty. Moreover, the "constitutional" rights conferred through this back door are far more expansive than those dreamed of by most property rights proponents.

Habitat Protection as Expropriation

The most obvious examples of how these rules will undermine the capacity of all governments to achieve environmental and planning objectives concern land-use controls and regulation. Whether it is for the purpose of preserving salmon habitat or to protect endangered species, the imposition of habitat protection measures can have significant impacts on the use of land subject to such protective measures.

For example, stream habitat protection measures can substantially limit the extent and character of forest harvesting activities. Similarly, land-use bylaws, agricultural land protection, parks creation, and other initiatives can impact development activity, whether occurring in remote or urban areas of the province.

By limiting the uses to which land may be put, the imposition of habitat protection measures can significantly reduce the development value of property or the profitability of harvesting licenses or other permits. But, according to NAFTA's expropriation rules, any government action that even indirectly interferes with the profitability of an investment may justify a claim for damages and compensation. Nor are there any exceptions to this prohibition against such government actions. While such measures are permitted when taken for legitimate public purposes, in every instance full compensation must be promptly paid to any foreign investor and for the full market value of any investment "expropriated". This is true no matter how compelling the public policy rationale for infringing investor rights.

Environmental and Public Health Regulation as Expropriation

It is also important to understand that this expropriation rule applies to the full range of economic interests that fall within the treaties' broad definition of investment. This means that an investor need not have a direct interest in real property to assert a claim for compensation. Because the MAI defines "expropriation" in the broadest terms, its rules may effectively prohibit a broad array of government regulations that even indirectly reduce the profitability of corporate investment.

In fact, it would be difficult to identify an environmental or conservation initiative that would not have this effect, at least for some investors. Indeed, there is recent evidence that environmental regulations are the most likely target of this prohibition against government "taking." One case in point is a lawsuit brought by Ethyl Corporation, a U.S.-based transnational, against the government of Canada. Because the suit was among the first to be brought under the investment rules of NAFTA, we have summarized the important details in the following box.

"Threat of NAFTA Case Kills Canada's MMT Ban"

Ethyl Corp., a U.S. multinational corporation, is the only North American manufacturer of MMT, a controversial manganese fuel additive. According to the auto industry, MMT damages pollution control systems, increasing emissions of VOCs, CO_2, and Carbon Monoxide. Like other heavy metals, MMT is also a neurotoxin, and its impacts on human health have not yet been adequately assessed.

In fact, understanding how exposure to airborne heavy metals damages human nervous systems is often very difficult. In the case of lead, it took more than 60 years to finally establish. This explains why many countries have relied on the "precautionary principle" to ban or restrict the use of MMT as a fuel additive.

While Ethyl denies that MMT is harmful to human health or the environment, this is the same corporation that stonewalled action on leaded gasoline for years.

When Environment Canada finally decided to regulate MMT in April 1996, it did so by banning the importation and inter-provincial transport of MMT. But no sooner was the bill proclaimed than Ethyl Corp. filed a claim under NAFTA's investment rules for $350 million in damages. Ethyl's suit alleged that, by effectively banning MMT, Canada had expropriated its business, and had violated the National Treatment and Performance Requirement provisions of NAFTA, as well.

Canadians learned of Ethyl's claim only because the company decided to make it public. When West Coast Environmental Law and other groups sought to intervene in the case, we were rebuffed by the Canadian government, which also denied access to any of the documents relating to the case, either Ethyl's or its own. Thus, during 1997 and early 1998, the case proceeded under the "cone of silence" imposed by NAFTA's highly secretive arbitration rules.

While federal officials publicly discounted Ethyl's claim, internal memoranda offered a more sober assessment.[90] In fact, the government was so concerned about losing the case that it decided to settle on terms that can only be considered a complete capitulation to Ethyl's claims.

On July 20, 1998, under the front page headline "Threat of NAFTA Case kills Canada's MMT Ban," the *Globe and Mail* reported that Canada had agreed to rescind the MMT ban, pay Ethyl in excess of $19 million, and take the unprecedented step of issuing a statement that MMT was neither an environmental nor a health risk. Not surprisingly, even prominent members of the Liberal government "slammed" the deal as a "sell-out of the public interest." [Southam Newspapers: "MPs defy colleagues on MMT," *Vancouver Sun*, July 24, 1998].

Thus, the first case to invoke the powerful enforcement rules of NAFTA resulted in a stunning victory for a U.S.-based transnational corporation unhappy with Canadian environmental regulation. Moreover, to avoid a whopping damage settlement, the federal government has set a dangerous precedent for similar challenges by other foreign investors.

Indeed, it is clear that other corporations have already got the message because Canada has recently been served with another claim by a U.S.-based corporation, S.D. Myers, for damages arising from a ban (since removed) on the international trade of PCB waste.

Even more chilling is the fact that federal officials have refused to disclose how many other lawsuits have been made under NAFTA's investment rules, arguing that even the fact that a claim has been made against the Canadian government is protected by the secrecy rules of NAFTA's dispute procedures.

More than one trade lawyer from the corporate sector has warned that there will be many more such suits as their clients make more frequent use of their rights under these investment treaties to "harass" governments contemplating regulatory initiatives that corporations oppose.

As disturbing as these developments are, they have brought to greater public attention the truly draconian rules for dispute resolution put in place by these investment treaties. Even the editorial boards of the *Globe and Mail* and the *Financial Post* have criticized the extraordinary and secretive character of these investor–state suits.[91]

We can also hope that the Ethyl case will spark long-overdue attention to NAFTA and the need to eliminate rules that expose Canadian laws and regulations to the withering fire of investor–state litigation.

5. Investor–State Procedures: A "Revolution" in International Law

Rarely is an agreement more effective than the enforcement mechanisms available to ensure that its terms are observed. For this reason, the most important provisions in the NAFTA and similar investment treaties are certain to be the ones with teeth, i.e., those that will compel governments to comply with its dictates. These can be found for example in Chapter 11 of NAFTA under the heading "Settlement of Disputes Between a Party and an Investor of Another Party."

The dispute settlement rules of NAFTA and the MAI were virtually identical and establish two distinct enforcement regimes to ensure that governments respect the new limits on their authority that these treaties establish. They are certain to be revived as central to proposals to expand investor rights under the WTO. These are: State–State Procedures and Investor–State Procedures. As we have noted elsewhere in this guide, State to State dispute processes are not without controversy, largely because they exclude public access and participation. However, these concerns pale by comparison with those raised by the Investor–State cases.

To begin, it is important to understand that, prior to NAFTA, only national governments had standing to invoke dispute resolution processes under international trade agreements. Under this arrangement, governments often refused to file trade complaints on behalf of domestic corporations upset by the policies and practices of other countries. But, under Investor–State procedures, the role of national governments as intermediaries is eliminated. NAFTA rules now allow foreign investors to sue national governments directly, and for any alleged breach of the very expansive and broadly-worded investor rights they are granted by these investment treaties.

These disputes are then decided, not by domestic courts or judges, but by international arbitration panels operating under the auspices of such institutions as the World Bank and the International Chamber of Commerce.

Arbitration panels do not follow domestic legal principles and procedures, but rather apply international legal rules and operate in accordance with procedures established for resolving international commercial disputes. Because these procedures are so highly secretive, they must be seen as antithetical to the principles of open, participatory, and democratic decision-making that are the hallmarks of contemporary legal systems.

For example, under these dispute rules, panel hearings are entirely closed to public view or participation. Nor is public access to documents or evidence permitted, unless both parties agree. In fact, as we have noted, the federal government has taken the position that it cannot even reveal whether a claim has been made against it under these procedures. Most astonishingly, under MAI rules, the "cone of silence" actually includes the decisions made by these international tribunals, even when they involve major damage awards against our government!

In addition to constituting a fundamental assault on the democratic traditions of Canadian law, these enforcement regimes also represent a radical departure from the norms of international law. First, they provide corporations with the right to directly enforce an international treaty to which they are not parties, and under which they have no obligations. Second, they extend international commercial arbitration to claims that have nothing to do with commercial contracts and everything to do with public policy and law. This is why even conservative legal experts have described these rules as representing a "revolutionary departure"[92] from the principles of international and Canadian law.

Many of us take for granted that we live in countries with open, democratic, and accountable judicial systems. We no doubt share the conviction that the public administration of justice is so fundamental to a democratic society that it would be unassailable in the contemporary political context. But, as even this overview makes clear, NAFTA has already established a regime for enforcing investor rights that has supplanted Canadian laws and courts with procedures that exist entirely outside the confines of the legal norms of our society. It would be very difficult to overstate the gravity of this challenge to the democratic process.

Environmental Conditionalities and Other Greenwash

In response to an environmental critique, defenders of these treaties will quickly point to various provisions that appear to reflect some willingness to accept that investment rights respect some environmental limits. For example, a provision of NAFTA's Investment Chapter states:

The Parties recognize that it is inappropriate to encourage investment by lowering domestic health, safety or environmental standards or relaxing domestic labour standards.

But, unlike other NAFTA investment rules, this provision is unenforceable and for that reason virtually meaningless—particularly in the context of a trade regime that encourages countries to compete for investment by allowing corporations to externalize environmental and other social costs.

Similarly, Performance Requirements include an "exception" that would allow governments to regulate, "where necessary,"

- to protect human, animal or plant life, or health, or

- for the conservation of living or non-living exhaustible natural resources.

Again, what isn't clear to those unfamiliar with the esoteric rules of trade agreements is that this is identical language to that used in a general exception to GATT rules, where it has proven to be virtually useless, as the case summaries included in this guide readily reveal.

Finally, it is important to recognize that, even should this environmental language prove to be far more effective than it has been in other trade agreements, it would still have no impact on the rule against "expropriation," because it simply has no application to this provision of the investment treaty.

Exceptions and Reservations

When it really matters, governments have been willing to create meaningful exceptions to treaty-based investor rights. For example, a broad and unequivocal exemption has been included in NAFTA, at the insistence of the U.S, for measures deemed necessary for the "protection of essential security interests." To this point, however, no government has been willing to argue that a similar exception is required for government actions deemed necessary for the protection of our essential ecological security.

In addition to this failure, and unlike NAFTA, under the WTO no general exception is allowed for measures taken to honour Canada's obligations under international environmental agreements—such as those needed to reduce greenhouse-gas emissions, protect biodiversity, or control trade in hazardous waste or endangered species.

Instead of proposing such exceptions, the federal government is offering only its assurance that it will "reserve" various policies and practices from the full application of these investment rules. There are, however, several reasons to discount these assurances as having little value. To begin with, the extent of reservations that Canada may claim is a subject for negotiation and compromise, so it may simply not get everything it has asked for. More to the point, environmental and many other vital issues are not even on Canada's list of proposed reservations.

Even if they were, the "standstill" rule that is common to these international agreements effectively precludes new policy or regulatory measures that might even marginally impair investor rights. This means that, even for most of the matters reserved, Canadian policy would be frozen in time, becoming increasingly obsolete and irrelevant with each passing day.

Furthermore, Canada is not even willing to discuss reservations from the most problematic investor rights. For example, of the Canadian reservations listed under NAFTA, not one applies to the Expropriation and Compensation rule. As we have noted, there is no other provision of this investment regime that is likely to be more destructive of public policy and legal prerogatives.

Similarly, with the single exception of the Investment Canada Act, no reservation is allowed from the dispute settlement provisions of NAFTA, including Investor–State Procedures. The same was true of proposals for the MAI, which provide the best guide to what is likely in store for WTO investment negotiations. Therefore, all other matters, including the effect of a listed reservation, are vulnerable to challenge pursuant to these procedures.

The demands of a growing number of such claims will easily overwhelm scarce and ever declining government resources. As has already occurred in the Ethyl case, the costs of litigation, together with the risks of losing a major claim, are simply intolerable, particularly when the expedient of simply eliminating offending regulations is available. More and more often, governments will simply opt for the safest course, which will be to avoid environmental and other regulatory initiatives altogether. In fact, we can already observe the pernicious effect of this new global reality as governments shed regulatory standards in favour of voluntary programs and initiatives.

Finally, on this subject, if reservations are broad enough to provide meaningful opportunity for progressive environmental reforms, they could undo much of what NAFTA and similar agreements are intended to accomplish. In seeking to entrench the dominant system of market-driven growth by reducing government's ability to regulate corporate activity in the public interest, these rules are on a collision course with the bedrock principles on which our environmental agenda is built.

The Need for New Investment Controls in the Era of Globalization

This analysis of NAFTA, the MAI, and present WTO proposals has focused on the need to preserve and even strengthen the capacity of our governments to regulate investors to ensure that in Canada they operate in a manner consistent with the broad public interest. But it is clear that we must also address the need for better controls on the foreign investment activities of the Canadian government and Canadian investors.

For example, the foreign subsidiaries of Canadian-based mining companies have recently been responsible for three major mine-tailings disasters.

The Ugly Canadian

This was the title of a recent CBC documentary describing the impacts associated with several spectacular environmental disasters caused by Canadian mining companies operating abroad, all of which have occurred during the last three years.

In Guyana, a spill of 860 million gallons of cyanide contaminated water from a Cambior site, affecting over 50 miles of primary river habitat upon which local citizens, farmers, and fishers depended.

In the Philippines, a holding system of a mine in which Placer Dome owns a 39.9% interest gave way, releasing over four million tons of mine waste into local rivers, with devastating consequences for local communities, five of which were eventually evacuated.

The most recent of these disasters occurred in Spain, where thousands of hectares of farmland and species habitat was devastated by a spill from Boliden's Los Freille operations in that country. Clean-up costs are estimated to be in excess of $100 million, and yet enhanced protection of these companies' rights in foreign countries is identified as one of the main reasons Canada is pursuing the MAI and other similar initiatives.

At the urging of Quebec's mining industry, the Canadian government has recently filed a trade challenge against France because it enacted strong asbestos regulations. Apparently the claim was motivated by a desire to protect the investments and markets of Quebec's asbestos industries in Southeast Asia, where governments might follow the French precedent should it be allowed to stand.

As another example, Canada recently exempted the sale of Candu nuclear reactors to China from federal environmental review. When Canadian investors, both public and private, are responsible for environmental damage in developing countries, local communities may have little if any recourse. However, even in developed countries foreign investors may simply decide to pull up stakes rather than face clean-up and compensation costs. Moreover, when the foreign victims of Canadian investors have attempted to gain compensation from them in Canadian courts, they have been rebuffed.

We need to find new ways to regulate the activities of our own investors abroad: not through voluntary codes of conduct, but through meaningful and enforceable domestic and international laws—laws that will be as effectively designed to protect the environment and our communities as agreements such as NAFTA are intent on protecting the interests of foreign investors. A good beginning would be to:

1. ensure that the foreign victims of Canadian investors have recourse under Canadian law;

2. require the investment activities of Canadian investors outside Canada be held to no lower standard of environmental review and performance than would be required of them in Canada;

3. mandate a process for public notice and comment before Canada files a trade complaint against another country's environmental or public health laws in response to behind-closed-door lobbying efforts by Canadian investors; and

4. establish enforceable international regimes to ensure that the investors comply with the lofty principles currently expressed in voluntary codes of international corporate conduct.

A Citizen's Agenda

If international investment rules are to foster, rather than undermine, our prospects for achieving environmental goals, they will have to be fundamentally overhauled. As noted in the report of the European Parliament that led to France withdrawing from MAI negotiations, it is the basic architecture of the MAI that is the problem.[93]

There is probably no better way to expose how far off the mark this regime is than to identify the investment policies and law needed to support the goals of environmental protection, resource conservation, and sustainable economic development. Unfortunately, the provisions of the Investment Chapter of NAFTA, and present proposals for expanding WTO investment rules, represent the antithesis of these principles.

1. All governments have the sovereign right to regulate the activities of both foreign and domestic investors to require their activities to conform to the public interest.

2. In no case are the rights of foreign investors to take precedence over the public policy goals of environmental protection, resource conservation, and sustainable development.

3. All governments have the sovereign right to ensure that the use of natural resources within their territories serve the imperatives of conservation and biodiversity and, secondarily, economic development in their communities. In all instances, governments and First Nations have the right to optimize the value of their resources to the particular benefit of their citizens and members.

4. Foreign investors must comply with the highest standards prevailing in either their home or host jurisdiction, whichever is higher.

5. All investor claims arising under any international agreement can proceed only at the instance of nation-states, and then only in accordance with the norms of notice, participation, and accountability that are fundamental to the judicial systems of democratic societies.

6. In the event of conflict with international environmental agreements, such as the Framework Convention on Climate Change, the Biodiversity Convention, and the Pacific Salmon Treaty, these agreements will prevail over the MAI.

7. Claims for compensation against Canada concerning expropriation shall proceed only in Canadian courts and in accordance with Canadian law.

In many ways, the alternative to the international investor-rights agenda means preserving the policies, laws and programs that it would eliminate. Because we have taken these for granted for so long, we have lost sight of the important public policy rationale for the measures that we now risk losing.

12

Health Care and Other Services

In this chapter, we consider the impact of the services regimes of both NAFTA and the WTO. As we shall see, the impact of the General Agreement on Trade in Services (the GATS) is broader than for any other housed within the WTO framework and extends well beyond the ambit of social services. The complexity of the GATS warrants a more in-depth review than is possible here, and fortunately there is an extensive and growing body of critical analysis which is now becoming available.[94] Therefore, rather than attempt a comprehensive assessment, this chapter examines how the services rules of the WTO and NAFTA are likely to determine the future of what is probably Canada's most important public service—health care.

In many ways, the trade liberalization objectives of the WTO and NAFTA services rules are fundamentally incompatible with policies that seek to exclude market forces in order to achieve other societal goals, such as the provision of universal and accessible publicly funded health care.

For example, the investment and services rules of these trade regimes seek to contain the capacity of governments to regulate or otherwise intervene in these spheres of the economy. On the other hand, Canada's health care system depends upon a comprehensive framework of federal and provincial policy, law and funding arrangements that restrict the rights of private investors and service providers in order to preserve a public health care system based on the five principles of the Canada Health Act: public administration, comprehensiveness, universality, portability, and accessibility.

By establishing a public sector health insurance monopoly and by regulating who can provide health care services and on what terms, the provisions of the Canada Health Act cut very much against the grain of the deregulation and privatization objectives of trade liberalization. Of particular concern is the failure of the WTO and NAFTA to recognize the validity of distinguishing between public and private services, rendering the former vulnerable to challenge as offending National Treatment requirements. Thus the policies, programs and regulatory framework created to support a public health care system are by their very nature discriminatory with respect to non-public and for-profit health care services.

These inherent and explicit contradictions between public health care and free trade explain why Canada needed to protect its health system from the full impact of trade disciplines. Ultimately, the future viability of Canada's public health care system depends upon the integrity and broad application of these safeguards.

However, in negotiating the WTO and NAFTA, Canada failed to insist upon broad exclusions for health care, relying instead on a patchwork of reservations and other technical strategies to shelter the Canadian system from the corrosive influence of international trade disciplines.

Unfortunately, an examination of the details of Canada's strategy reveals it to be fraught with ambiguity and uncertainty. This leads to the uncomfortable conclusion that Canada's piecemeal and qualified approach creates real vulnerability for the framework of Canadian health care policy under both WTO and NAFTA rules.

A few facts about this cornerstone of Canadian social policy will help explain how our health care system is put at risk by NAFTA and WTO disciplines concerning investment and services.

Canada's Mixed Health Care System

Canada's health care system is a mix of public and private sector service delivery. Most physicians providing insured medical services operate private for-profit businesses subject to certain regulatory controls, e.g., licensing and extra billing. On the other hand, most hospitals in Canada delivering insured medical services are not-for-profit institutions, of which many are operated by religious or charitable foundations. However, a number of private hospitals and clinics also exist in Canada providing services that fall both within and outside of the Medicare funding umbrella.

The landscape of Canadian health care continues to evolve, but often in ways that are hardly conducive to maintaining a robust and durable public health care system. The Honourable Monique Bégin, who is one of the architects of our system, recently described the gradual erosion of Canadian health care through:

Surreptitious de-listing or de-insurance of services by provincial governments; private clinics operating both in and out of provincial plans for "medically necessary services" (and their medical practitioners keeping hospital privileges and having it both ways); treating GPs or specialists directing their patients to private labs and clinics for regular procedures for the full out-of-pocket cost; hospitals charging partial costs for exams because these might not be "medically necessary" (wanting a MRI is not like choosing to have a hair colouring!). These are all erosions of Medicare. People started losing all sense of their entitlements to health care.[95]

The allegation implicit in this assessment is that Canada has been complicit in allowing the foundations of the health care system to be undermined. As part of the process, services that were once clearly part of the public system have been removed from it. In other words, the map of the Canadian health care system is continually being redrawn in ways that are ever diminishing the domain of public sector health care.

But, as we shall see, in large measure the protection afforded Canadian health care under NAFTA and the WTO depends upon maintaining the integrity of our system as a publicly funded social service, unadulterated by privatization and competitive service delivery. Moreover, as elements of our system are privatized and eroded, trade constraints will make it virtually impossible for them to be recovered.

Because the most likely assault on Canadian health care will come from U.S.-based health services corporations, it is important to assess the vulnerability of Canadian health care systems to challenges under both NAFTA and the WTO. These are considered in turn.

NAFTA's Free Trade Agenda and Public Health Care

As noted, in negotiating NAFTA, Canada failed to insist upon a broad exclusion for health care, relying instead upon the more limited protection of certain "reservations"[96] and on exceptions for government procurement and funding. Its decision to choose this course unnecessarily exposes our health care system to NAFTA disciplines.

For example, an exception for public health care would have applied to all NAFTA parties and been set out in the treaty's text. The broad and unqualified carve-out for *National Security* offers a good example. On the other hand, a reservation applies only to the country declaring it, and is usually found in an annex or supplementary document to the main text, as is the case for health under NAFTA. Moreover, exceptions are included as permanent features of the agreement, while reservations are often subject to the expectation that they will gradually be removed over time.[97]

To further exacerbate these difficulties, the actual way in which Canada has established a reservation under NAFTA for health care[98] is qualified and ambiguous because it only applies to health services "to the extent that they are social services established or maintained for a public purpose." But the U.S. and Canada have very different views about what this qualification really means. Thus, the U.S. Trade Representative described a U.S. reservation identical to Canada's as

> intended to cover services which are similar to those provided by a government, such as child care or drug treatment programs. If those services are supplied by a private firm, on a profit or not-for-profit basis, Chapter Eleven and Chapter Twelve apply. Chapters 11 and 12 set out NAFTA investment and services provisions, respectively.

Because our health care system engenders many private for-profit elements, this U.S. view would render much of it exposed to NAFTA disciplines and the ambitions of U.S.-based investors and service providers. All of this was recently brought into sharp focus when Ralph Klein's government in Alberta decided to privatize the delivery of certain health care services under the rubric of "protecting" our health care system.

Health Care Protection—Ralph Klein Style

Bill 11, the *Health Care Protection Act*, was introduced by the government of Alberta on March 2, 2000. Advancing the cause of privatization under the banner of "health care protection," the Bill actually undermined public health care service delivery in that province by providing for-profit companies an unprecedented opportunity to participate in the delivery of publicly-funded health services. As the *Globe and Mail* described it: "Alberta will be the first province to entrench a large-scale private component in its public health care system."

But, as we have seen, Canada's ability to protect public health care may well depend upon its determination to keep private sector participation at bay. For, if the U.S. view prevails, once private firms are involved, Canada's reservation for health services simply has no application. Apparently sharing this concern, the federal Minister of Health put it this way in a letter to his provincial counterpart in Alberta:[99]

> Some have suggested that permitting private hospitals in Alberta which would be paid for by the public purse would encourage American firms to seek to establish similar hospitals within your jurisdiction. Further, it has been suggested that attempting to keep out such enterprises, or refusing to send them patients, may run afoul of provisions of NAFTA. Have you considered a strategy to deal with this potential problem?

Evading the issue, and notwithstanding widespread public dissatisfaction with his proposals, Alberta's premier decided to forge ahead with his plans. It now remains to be seen how successful Alberta's privatization initiative will be in assigning core health care services to the private sector, and whether other Canadian provinces decide to follow suit. There can be no doubt, however, that the privatization of insured health care services in Alberta will play directly to U.S. arguments and compromise the protection afforded by vital Canadian reservations.

But it is not only the exposure of public health care to NAFTA disciplines that is of concern, as we shall next see.

The General Agreement on Trade in Services (the GATS)

The immediate threat to public health care now looming on the WTO horizon has to do with efforts to complete the rudimentary framework established by the the General Agreement on Trade in Services (the GATS). Like the Multi-lateral Agreement on Investment (the MAI) which it closely resembles, the GATS represents an ambitious program to expand the application of international trade disciplines to a vast array of domestic policy, programs, and laws that may have very little, and often nothing, to do with international trade at all.

This assault on domestic policy prerogatives under the rubric of trade liberalization is made even more intrusive by the abandonment of the pretext that fairness or non-discrimination is the concern that justifies such an intervention. For, under GATS rules, the entire spectrum of service sector regulation is subject to trade disciplines, however non-discriminatory or even-handed their design or application. In this way, the coercive disciplines of international trade sanctions are made available to restrain non-discriminatory domestic policy and legislative initiatives, even at the most local level.

Bananas, Car Parts, and Health Care

Mention services to a typical Canadian and the notion of public services—health care; education; municipal water, sewage and waste services—will immediately come to mind. But under the GATS the range of government measures subject to these particular trade disciplines is far broader than those concerning public services. In fact, the GATS played a key role in two WTO disputes concerning the use of preferential tariffs on goods. The first involved a successful challenge to Canada's Auto Pact, which we describe in Chapter 9: Workers' Rights. The other, was a successful challenge by the U.S. to the Lome Convention, under which European countries provide preferrential access for some goods produced by its former colonies—in this case, bananas.

An understanding of how the GATS might have come into play in a dispute about trade in goods requires an appreciation of how broadly the concept of services has been defined under the WTO. To begin with, consider that a service might be defined as anything you can't drop on your foot. Heart surgery, hazardous waste treatment, advertising, water treatment, home care for the elderly, banking, logging, funerals, and shipping are all services and provide some sense of how broad and diverse this sphere of economic activity is.

But it is also possible to conceive of physical goods and products as the embodiment of the services (design, harvesting, marketing, etc.) that are the necessary elements of their production, distribution and sale. As the Auto Pact and Bananas trade cases illustrate, it is this broader conception that is relevant to understanding the full reach of the GATS.

That GATS rules have been given such broad application follows logically from the expansive way in which "services" has been defined by this agreement. To begin with, the GATS applies to all services except those supplied in the exercise of government authority—a term which Article 1.3(c) defines this way:

a service supplied *in the exercise of governmental authority* means any service which is supplied neither on a commercial basis, nor in competition with one or more service suppliers. [emphasis added]

Thus, the only service exempt from GATS disciplines are those provided by governments within these narrow parameters. This would exclude any public sector service which is offered either on a commercial basis (e.g., public utilities) or in competition with the private sector (waste management, water supply). In the modern era, where public services often represent a mix of monopolized and competitive services, it would be difficult to identify a public service that would be exempt pursuant to this definition—including public health care.

But apparently the federal government is relying upon this exclusion to protect public health care from GATS disciplines, and has declined an opportunity to list health care as an exception under this agreement. But, as we have seen, ever increasingly Canadian health care is either being provided on a commercial basis or in competition with the private sector. Consider in this light Alberta's decision to facilitate private, for-profit service delivery of one of the few remaining areas of health care still reserved to the public sector: surgical services requiring overnight hospital care.

However, while the ambition of the GATS is ultimately to establish a comprehensive code that will apply to all services, several of this agreement's more onerous provisions apply only to services which have been specifically committed (voluntarily submitted to GATS disciplines) by a particular country.

Nevertheless, several GATS obligations attach to all services unless otherwise exempt pursuant to Article 1.3 (c), or otherwise listed as an exception—an option which, as noted, Canada declined. This means that, with the possible exception of public health care insurance schemes, it would be difficult to identify any facet of our health care system that would fall within the parameters of this exclusion from GATS disciplines, and therefore be exempt from them. The issue of health insurance arises when we consider the sector-specific commitments which Canada has made under the GATS.

It is unclear at this point whether Canada's decision not to list health care as an exception under the GATS is the result of some terrible miscalculation about the ambit of this agreement or the parameters of Article 1.3 (c). If this indeed is the case, it won't be the first error Canada has made in comprehending the nature of the commitments that it has made under the WTO.[100] It would however, be the most serious.

Returning again to the general framework of the GATS, it is important also that this agreement applies to government policies, programs and laws, whether these are explicitly about services or not. This is given formal expression in two key GATS Articles. Article 1 provides:

> This Agreement applies to *measures* by Members *affecting trade* in services.

Similarly, the term "measures" is given an equally expansive definition by Article XXVIII:

> "measure" means any measure by a Member, whether in the form of a law, regulation, rule, procedure, decision, administrative action, or any other form...

While of limited relevance to the issue of health care, it is worth returning briefly to those two trade cases. Taking their cue from the expansive way in which the reach of this agreement has been defined, WTO dispute bodies have explained that, for a government measure to offend GATS constraints, it need not be about services at all. Thus, because government measures concerning the production and trade in bananas or automobiles impact related marketing, distribution, and sales services, such measures must respect the constraints imposed by this services agreement.[101]

In fact, most if not all product-specific regulations will have at least an incidental impact on related services (e.g., transportation, marketing, advertising). For this reason, it would be difficult to identify any government policy, program, law or regulation that might not be caught within the ambit of GATS disciplines.

Finally, with respect to the application of the GATS, it is important to note that it not only binds all levels of government, but Article 1.3 also seeks to constrain the activities of:

> non-governmental bodies in the exercise of powers delegated by central, regional or local governments or authorities...

This would include many of the functions the College of Physicians and Surgeons and many health-care-related agencies that are now bound to respect the limits imposed on their authority under the GATS. Remember, as well, that the delegation of authority to such bodies need not be a formal one because of the very broad definition given the term "measures."

De-regulation, Privatization, and Free Trade

Another key to understanding the full implications of the GATS requires that one shed two understandable assumptions that might be made about an international agreement which purports to be about trade and services. The first is that the agreement is primarily concerned with international trade in services. The second is that its essential thrust would be to prevent discriminatory treatment of foreign service providers.

While both of these principles represent important features of this international regime, a primary focus of the GATS is clearly on domestic policies, programs, and regulations. Moreover, in seeking to constrain such government initiatives, the essential objective of GATS disciplines is deregulation, not fairness. In fact, the impact of the GATS on services trade is arguably of less importance than its goal of permanently reducing the role of government, both as regulator and service provider. This, of course, is the now familiar agenda of deregulation and privatization, which for many of the advocates of trade "liberalization" are the most important benefits to be derived from agreements such as the GATS.[102]

No doubt these assertions will appear controversial to some. Again we can turn to the text of the agreement itself to test their validity.

Domestic Policy, Programs, and Law, Not International Trade Regulation

With the advent of modern telecommunications technology and integrated global systems of production and trade, it has become increasingly possible to deliver a growing array of services across international boundaries. Data management of health care records, and even hospital food services, are examples. But the largest proportion of services are still delivered on a local basis, and this is the case for most medical services as well. Because most services are still provided by local suppliers to local consumers, the impact of GATS disciplines will be much more broadly felt in the domain of domestic policy, programs, and law than in the area of international trade regulation.

To be sure, certain GATS rules are directed at international trade in services. But to achieve the goal of comprehensive coverage, many GATS disciplines apply to government measures concerning services, whether these are trade-related or not. This is described in the jargon of GATS as "modal neutrality," which seeks to capture any and all government measures concerning services, however local these initiatives may be in design and application. Accordingly, while the GATS applies putatively to government measures which affect "trade in services," that term is defined by Article 1.2 to include four modes of service delivery:

- from the territory of one Member into the territory of any other Member [cross–border];

- in the territory of one Member to the service consumer of any other Member [to consumers abroad];

- by a service supplier of one Member, through commercial presence in the territory of any other Member [commercial presence]; and

- by a service supplier of one Member, through presence of natural persons of a Member in the territory of any other Member [presence of natural persons].

Obviously, only one of these modes of services delivery actually involves cross-border trade in services. Moreover, the right of establishment engendered by sub-section (c) is really an investment measure more than anything else, and explains why the WTO touts the GATS as the first multilateral agreement on investment.[103]

Therefore, both the character of the services sector of the economy and the explicit provisions of the GATS lead to the inescapable conclusion that, notwithstanding the claim that it is an agreement about Trade in Services, the GATS is more concerned with domestic regulation than it is with international trade.

De-regulation, Not Fairness

As we know, the first principles of all WTO Agreements are those of National Treatment and Most Favoured Nation Treatment. These bulwarks of free trade are also set out in the GATS. But this particular WTO Agreement goes well beyond the principle of non-discrimination by prohibiting a broad array of government policies, programs, practices, and laws, however equitably these may be applied. It would be difficult to overstate the significance of this departure from, and expansion of, the basic framework of international trade agreements.

Thus, several of the GATS' most important articles impose a blanket prohibition against—or strict limits upon—policies, programs and laws, no matter how fair or even-handed their conception or application. These include:

Article III Transparency: effectively establishes an international notice and comment regime whereby all nations must publish promptly... "all relevant measures of general application which pertain to or affect... services, and provide inquiry points for those seeking more information." This provision will alert foreign services providers to initiatives they may wish to lobby against, or failing which, persuade a sympathetic government to challenge.

Article VI Domestic Regulation: imposes a number of onerous tests which must be met by non-discriminatory domestic measures of general application. Notwithstanding their inherent fairness, such initiatives are prohibited unless: they are based on objective and transparent criteria; are no more "burdensome than necessary;" do not, in the case of licensing, restrict the supply of the service; and are administered in a reasonable, objective, and impartial manner.

Article VIII Monopolies: this provisions require that monopolies—in Canadian parlance, Crown corporations, municipal utilities, and other others licensed to provide exclusive services—comply with the constraints imposed by the GATS and not abuse [their] monopoly position.

Article XVI Market Access: this provision prohibits six different types of regulatory controls which might otherwise apply to the provision of services. These include:

a) limitations on the number of service suppliers;

b) limitations on the total value of service transactions;

c) limitations on the total number of service operations;

d) limitations on the total number of natural persons that may be employed in a particular service sector;

e) measures which restrict or require specific types of legal entity or joint venture through which a service supplier may supply a service; and

f) limitations on the participation of foreign capital in terms of maximum percentage limit on foreign shareholding or the total value of individual or aggregate foreign investment.

Some of these obligations apply to services across the board, unless explicitly exempt from GATS disciplines. Others apply only to services with respect to which specific commitments have been made. However, where they apply, it is to simply prohibit all measures, discriminatory or not, once these are captured by the broad framework of GATS disciplines. This obviously goes far beyond free trade policy designed to prohibit discriminatory practices which may inhibit trade. Rather, the GATS directly expresses an agenda for deregulation which uses the convenient vehicle of an international agreement in order to enlist the coercive discipline of trade sanctions to compel governments to abandon whole spheres of domestic policy and regulatory initiative.

Privatization, Not Trade

The privatization or "pro-competitive" bias of the WTO is apparent throughout its discussion papers and background notes,[104] but the privatization objectives of the GATS are woven into the fabric of this trade regime in a manner that is subtle and indirect. Thus, with one exception, no provision of the GATS squarely challenges the right of governments to choose or maintain public sector health care services. For the most part, the assault is rather upon the underlying policies, programs, regulatory and funding arrangements upon which the maintenance of public services depends. In point form, here is a list of the key GATS provisions that will, if left unchecked, lead to the privatization of most public services.

Article VIII: Monopolies and Exclusive Service Suppliers: This provision imposes many of the same constraints on public sector service providers that limit the options of government. Public sector service providers are also enjoined by this rule from "abusing" their monopoly position by acting in a manner inconsistent with GATS rules.[105] Furthermore, sub-section 4 of this Article effectively requires that private sector service providers be compensated where monopoly rights are created with respect to the supply of service. It is this last element that will make it impossible for a government to retrace its steps should any privatization initiative produce less than desirable results.

Article XVI Market Access: Maintaining certain public services as local, provincial or national monopolies obviously and directly impedes market access by foreign service providers. If the GATS' Market Access provisions are deemed to require no more than National Treatment, then such monopolies may be consistent with GATS requirements if they discriminate against foreign service providers to no greater extent than they impact their domestic private sector counterparts.[106] However, the wording of this Article clearly indicates that Market Access obligations require more than National Treatment. This would raise serious questions about the entire framework within which health care service monopolies exist. Moreover, where Market Access commitments have been made (see discussion of health insurance below) sub-section (e) of this Article prohibits "measures which restrict or require specific types of legal entity or joint venture through which a service supplier may supply a service." This would apparently preclude any specification that particular services be provided by not-for-profit public sector hospitals, for example.

Article XVII National Treatment: This provision requires the Canadian government or agency to accord foreign service providers treatment "no less favourable than it accords to its own like services and service suppliers." By failing to distinguish between private and public sector services suppliers, the GATS refuses to provide any latitude for policies, programs and regulations which may explicitly or effectively favour public sector service providers.

It is beyond the ambit of this paper to explore the various ways in which these provisions may be enlisted in support of the privatization goals that are such a central feature of neoliberal economic policies. A more detailed consideration of GATS reservations,[107] the role of procurement, and WTO subsidies disciplines would have to be part of such an assessment.

But one thing is clear, even from a superficial review of the history of this trade regime: there has been no meaningful public discussion of what these trade disciplines ultimately mean for the future of public health care. As has been the case for virtually every other element of the WTO, the rules of trade have been crafted without any assessment of their broader implications.

Health Care Services

The application of GATS rules to health care services depends, as noted, upon the extent to which Canada has agreed to submit them to the disciplines of this agreement. As we have seen, certain GATS provisions apply to all services unless delivered in the exercise of government authority. Thus, Most Favoured Nation, Transparency, and the Monopoly rules apply to all such services. The application of other GATS disciplines, however, depends upon the extent to which these services are listed in country-specific schedules. When a service is listed, the country is said to have made a specific commitment with respect to that service sector.

The listing process is complicated and allows a country to specify which precise GATS disciplines it is willing to embrace with respect to a particular sector. Commitments fall into three broad categories: Market Access, National Treatment and Additional Commitments. Moreover, with respect to each of these provisions, a country may qualify or limit its commitments to: certain modes of supply (e.g., cross-border); a certain time frame; or, with respect to particular types of regulatory elements (e.g., controls on the number of service suppliers).

While the complexity of this regime provides ample opportunity for missteps, correcting an error is difficult and likely to be costly. In all of this, a country is to be guided by GATS classification schedules which characterize services as belonging to particular sectors or sub-sectors.

Therefore, in order to assess the likely impact of the GATS on health care services, it is crucial to understand the GATS classification system, and then to assess the extent to which Canada has made commitments in relevant service sectors.

Under the GATS, countries are free to classify their service sectors as they choose. But, given the complexity of classification and the potential for conflicts, many have chosen a system of classification established under the United Nations Statistics Divisions, called the Revised Central Product Code (CPC). This is the regime adopted by Canada.

There are twelve major headings of this classification system, one of which is Health and Social Services. Canada has made no commitments under this heading, which in fact doesn't even appear in its Schedule of Specific Commitments. One might at this point sigh in relief. Unfortunately, that would be premature in light of the potential impact of commitments Canada has made under other sector classifications on the delivery of health services.

For example, one area of emerging health care service delivery is now known as telemedicine. Thus, telecommunications advances, and in particular the Internet, have enabled remote monitoring, diagnosis and treatment of patients who may only occasionally, and perhaps never, actually meet their physician. In fact, in announcing a $1 billion program to ensure high-speed Internet connectivity for all Canadians, access to health services was identified as a prominent rationale for such a commitment.[108] It is clear however that technological innovation has already made the provision of medical services possible in ways that were not even imagined until a few years ago. Among these new capabilities is the cross-border supply of telemedical services to Canadians by private for-profit U.S.-based health care corporations.

While Canada has declined to make specific commitments concerning health care, it has made commitments under the heading Telecommunications Services. These include on-line information and database retrieval, electronic data interchange, and on-line information and/or data processing. Yet these are precisely the processes involved in providing telemedical services. The question, then, is whether Canada may have inadvertently exposed this new dimension of health care service delivery to GATS disciplines. Or, put another way, the policy options concerning the extent to which telemedical services are to be used, and who would be licensed to provide them, may have been foreclosed or significantly limited by Canada's listing of telecommunications services in its schedule of GATS commitments.

We simply cannot know at this juncture how a WTO dispute panel would resolve the latent conflicts that reside in the labyrinth of service sector classifications and literally thousands of sub-classifications. In the Auto Pact case, a listing error concerning wholesale auto sales played a key role in undoing Canada's most successful industrial strategy. It would be imprudent to assume that a similar fate might not befall Canadian health care.

Moreover, telecommunications services are not the only listings in Canada's schedule that may have the unintended effect of exposing public health care to the harsh disciplines of GATS rules. Engineering services (medical technology), computer and related services (see health care records management), management consulting services (hospital administration), and technical testing and analysis (medical laboratories) all have the potential for creating unforeseen consequences for health care services delivery.

But the most problemmatic potential conflict that may flow from commitments our federal government has made under the GATS concerns its listing of health insurance services under the heading Financial Services. As many will know, Canada's public health care system is in fact a publicly-financed health insurance system. Thus, the Canada Health Act stipulates the criteria that provincial health insurance plans must meet in order for a province to qualify for its full federal transfer payments.

But provinces and territories have primary responsibility for delivering health care services, and may provide coverage for services that fall outside of the national health insurance framework. In addition, a great deal of private health care insurance is also available to cover supplementary health services, but under provincial laws insurers are restricted from offering coverage which duplicates that of government programs.

In creating a public sector monopoly, regulating fees, and restricting the services that private insurers can provide, Canada's health care system cuts very much against the deregulation and privatization grain that the GATS and other WTO agreements were established to promote. Therefore, a listing of health insurance would bring our public insurance scheme potentially into conflict with GATS Market Access, Domestic Regulation, National Treatment, and Monopolies provisions—unless, that is, it is somehow absolved from meeting these obligations.

To make that determination requires a careful analysis of the Annex on Financial Services to the GATS which broadens the ambit of the definition set out in Article I.3(b) concerning "services supplied in the exercise of government authority" to include "activities conducted by a public entity for the account or with the guarantee or using the financial resources of the Government."[109] This may indeed broaden the ambit of this exclusion from GATS disciplines sufficientlty to shelter public health insurance.

However, this picture is muddied by an Understanding on Commitments in Financial Services (the Understanding) which was also included as part of the WTO framework. The Understanding is not to be confused with the Agreement on Financial Services, which is also part of the WTO regime.

The Understanding includes the requirement that "each member list in its schedule pertaining to financial services existing monopoly rights and shall endeavour to eliminate them or reduce their scope." This provision explicitly applies to activities referred to in Article 1.3(b) of the Annex (noted above). Yet public health care insurance is not listed by Canada as a monopoly with respect to its listing of health insurance. Apparently, this decision was based on the view that the health care insurance monopolies mandated by the Canada Health Act are otherwise excluded under Article I of the GATS itself.

If your head isn't swimming by now, you might qualify for a position at WTO headquarters in Geneva. The point of citing these provisions has not been to provide a thorough assessment of the implications for our health care system of Canada's decision to list health insurance. That would take a book of its own, and, if the issue is ever litigated, a WTO dispute panel will no doubt take several hundred pages to present its conlusions. Lengthy decisions are now the norm as the complexity of WTO agreements, relative to the GATT, have increased exponentially.

Rather, the point has been to illustrate just how complex the GATS and its attendant annexes, agreements, and understandings are. It may be that Canada's listing of health insurance under the GATS will not have any adverse or unexpected impacts on the integrity of the current system. But this will depend upon Canada's expertise in negotiating the uncharted labyrinth of the WTO's most complex Agreement. Unfortunately, Canada's record in this regard is hardly encouraging.

If this history with the GATs reveals anything, it is that there are many pitfalls and traps into which public policy may dissappear, even if indirectly impeding the trade liberalization objectives of this agreement. All of this only serves to underscore the difficulties

associated with Canada's failure to establish a blanket exclusion for
health care under the GATS.

The only thing in all of this that is certain is that, if a challenge to
our health care system is made under the GATS, the final judgment
will rest with the unelected and unaccountable adjudicators of WTO
dispute bodies. None would be Canadian, and none would need to
have any experience or familiarity with our public health care system. Moreover, the defense of Canadian policy will rest with the
same government department that is responsible for negotiating these
agreements in the first place. It is difficult in these circumstances to
be confident about the future of public health care in Canada, so long
as the contradictions with our international trade obligations remain
unaddressed.

Is There a Need for an International Services Agreement?

We have attempted to highlight the ways in which the GATS represents an astonishing departure from the tenets of free trade by actually prohibiting non-discriminatory domestic measures that may
have no meaningful impact on international trade in services whatsoever. But there is another way in which the GATS can be distin-
guished from the GATT: because, unlike international trade in goods,
there is simply no plausible rationale for an international agreement
about services. This is why:

1. Notwithstanding the new technologies and the globalization
   of production and trade, most services are still delivered on a
   local basis. For this reason, an international agreement about
   services is inherently invasive of domestic policy and law. Indeed, it is the corporate ambition to extend the reach of international disciplines to domestic, non-trade-related, and
   non-discriminatory measures that may be seen as the fundamental rationale for a services agreement. If the GATS were
   actually limited to international trade in services, corporate
   enthusiasm for this project would no doubt greatly diminish.

2. It is very difficult to identify a rationale for such a services
   agreement. While some possible justifications come to
   mind—e.g., the need to regulate international trade in hazardous waste services—this objective can just as readily be
   achieved by regulating trade in goods, or in this case "bads."

Moreover, by focusing on the trans-boundary transaction rather than domestic facilities, or lack thereof, border measures become sufficient and obviate the need to meddle in domestic environmental policy and law. Moreover, agreements such as the Basel Convention of Hazardous Waste Trade should not be housed within the WTO framework anyway. In addition, there is also virtue in keeping our international commitments as clear as possible. We have seen how the redundancy of WTO agreements has served global corporate interests in the Auto Pact, Split-Run Magazine, and Bananas cases. We should be leery of replicating this approach because uncertainty is itself corrosive of sovereign authority. If an agreement about hazardous waste exports is sufficient, then we need not bolster it with an agreeement about hazardous waste services as well.

It is simply very difficult to identify a justifiable rationale for ceding sovereignty, even were one to imagine an ideal international services agreement.

We have for the sake of this analysis used public health care as the vantage point from which to assess the potential impact of the GATS on all services. However, as we have seen, the expansive way in which the term "services" has been defined will mean that the reach of these particular trade disciplines will be far broader than any conventional understanding of services would imply. Because it constrains non-discriminatory domestic policy and law, this particular WTO agreement is far more corrosive of sovereign authority than any other. But the GATS framework is far from complete and is, at this writing, very much the subject of ongoing negotiations.

This offers a critical opportunity for Canadians to hold their elected representatives accountable for the commitments that have been made in their name. Those who are members of government should be encouraged to explain why it was worth gambling with the future of Medicare in order to further the interests of domestic service industries that might have foreign investment and trade ambitions and not be content to pursue the ample opportunities that already exist to further these interests.

13

Conclusions

In a disturbing analysis of what he describes as the two emergent forces in the world—consumer capitalism and religious fundamentalism—Benjamine Barber describes how the interrelationship between McWorld and Jihad is working to undermine democratic institutions and the nation-state upon which they depend.

The antipathy of religious and tribal fundamental groups to democratic governments is, he argues, born of their view that such governments are both a source of secular—read, heretical—authority, as well as a threat to maintaining the purity of tribal or ethnic communities.

As for the impacts of McWorld on civil society, Barber puts it this way:

> There is no activity more intrinsically globalizing than trade, no ideology less interested in nations than capitalism, no challenge to frontiers more audacious than the market. By many measures, corporations are today more central players in global affairs than nations. We call them multinational, but they are more accurately understood as transnational or post-national or anti-national. For they abjure the very idea of nations or any other parochialism that limits them in time or space. Their customers are not citizens or a particular nation or members of a parochial clan: they belong to the universal tribe of consumers defined by needs and wants that are ubiquitous, if not by nature then by cunning or advertising. A consumer is a consumer is a consumer.[110]

This guide is essentially about one of these two ascendant forces: globalization. It has attempted to expose how corporate imperatives have led to the establishment of international trade regimes designed to remove the few remaining impediments to full integration of global production and distribution systems, and place them firmly in the grasp of a handful of very large corporations. The most important of these obstacles, of course, is the capacity of nation-states to regulate and tax corporations to protect workers or the environment; to preserve diversity, both cultural and economic; to support basic public infrastructure and services; or to any other public purpose.

Another significant impediment to corporate ambition is the role of governments as providers of services—e.g., health care, education, water, and so on—which would otherwise represent new business and growth opportunities for the private sector. Hence the rallying cry of business groups: deregulation, privatization, and free trade! As we have seen, the WTO and its antecedent agreements such as NAFTA provide a faithful codification of these corporate objectives.

As we have also described, the WTO represents a revolutionary departure from the fundamental characteristics of the trade agreements it has replaced. These had traditionally been restricted in scope to facilitating consensual resolution of disputes concerning trade in goods or commodities. But, under the WTO, trade rules are now binding. Indeed, as the case studies and anecdotes presented here reveal, the invisible hand of the market has now become an iron fist, ensuring that all nations heed the new constraints that have been imposed on the exercise of public authority.

Moreover, with the expansion of the traditional scope of trade agreements to include rules about standards, investment, services, and intellectual property, the WTO rules apply to a greatly expanded realm of public policy and law that often will have nothing to do with trade at all.

It is clear that the WTO is a watershed in the evolution of international trade agreements in aid of formalizing and entrenching the conditions upon which globalization depends. Indeed, because of the breadth of its application and the enforcement mechanisms available to ensure that its rules are observed, it is not unrealistic to regard the WTO as the first effective world government in human history.

We have also described how the rules of this global government were written behind closed doors and guided almost exclusively by the single-minded preoccupations of the world's largest corporations. Not only was civil society excluded from trade negotiations, but the mystique and complexity of international trade issues often allowed trade bureaucrats to operate with very little political oversight. In most cases, when the prerogatives of government relating to health care, culture, and environmental protection were being discussed, the Ministers responsible for these matters simply deferred to the trade experts, even when on rare occasions they were invited to express their views.

One might be forgiven for discerning in all of this some diabolical corporate conspiracy to defeat democratic process and governance. Indeed, according to one of the most senior trade officials in the world, the norms of trade negotiations are not so much indifferent to democratic process as they are hostile to it.[111] But there is a more benign interpretation that may be more accurate: The assault on government sovereignty that is undeniably the pith and substance of the WTO is simply the inevitable consequence of the corporate imperative to remove any and all impediments to further growth in the new global context.

While multinational corporations have existed for many years, the advent of truly global and integrated production and distribution systems—globalization—is a relatively recent phenomenon, largely made possible by the telecomunications advances of the last few decades. Products are no longer made in particular places for particular markets: they are made everywhere and for everyone who can afford them. From this global corporate perspective, national regulation is extremely problematic: in a world of fickle capital investment and volatile stock markets, any government regulation can undermine the imperative to maximize growth and profits. More importantly, laws and regulations that differ from place to place are incompatible with free capital flows and the integrated production of commodities and products for global markets.

That is why the thrust of modern trade and investment agreements is to reduce, and even eliminate, the capacity of national and local governments to regulate the corporate sector. It matters not whether the purpose of that regulation is to protect the environment, provide public health care, preserve biodiversity, conserve natural resources, promote sustainable economic development, or accomplish other societal goals.

The detrimental effects of this corporate agenda on democratic institutions, the environment, public health, and other societal values are unlikely to have been planned, and may not have even been foreseen. The inevitable logic of globalization simply dictates a script that trade officials blindly follow. True, there are ideological warriors of the right, such as the Fraser Institute, that relish any opportunity to attack institutions of the state. But ideology probably has very little to do with the real world of trade negotiations. Indeed, when the precepts of free markets interfere with corporate objectives—as they clearly do in the case of patent rights—the principle of deregulation is quickly abandoned in favour of strong state controls to protect corporate interests.

Whatever the motivations, it seems clear that we have entrenched, as a global constitution, economic and trade policies that will fundamentally undermine the capacity of governments to address the pressing social, economic, and environmental problems that loom before us. It will be of no consolation that the severe and global consequences of this agenda may have been inadvertent.

Throughout, this guide has used an environmental lens through which to observe and evaluate the impacts of globalization and the free trade agenda. While there is room for debate about the precepts of globalization in terms of macroeconomic policy, it is impossible to reconcile the principles of unregulated growth and specialized global production with the two most pressing imperatives of this time: combatting global warming and preserving biodiversity.

There is now a very broad scientific consensus that substantial reductions in greenhouse-gas emissions will be required over the next few decades if we are to avert global climate change that is both unpredictable and potentially catastrophic. A disturbing and similar consensus exists about the need for dramatic measures to halt what a majority of biologists now believe to be the early stages of the sixth great mass extinction of life on Earth—this one, man-made. Yet the WTO entrenches the very dynamics of economic development that must be seen as the root cause of these ecological crises, while at the same time removing from governments the tools that will be needed to change our present course.

No matter how daunting our prospects, however, we now have a critical opportunity to develop alternative models for economic and social development—models that are just, socially responsible, and ecologically viable. If we are to succeed in meeting these challenges, we will have to probe beneath the symptoms of destructive and unsustainable development policies, and confront the underlying economic and trade policies that drive them.

Throughout this guide, we have attempted to describe the transformation of trade policies and trade agreements that will be needed if we are to set this new course. To be sure, the challenge of bringing about these dramatic reforms is truly formidable. So, rather than attempting to summarize these proscriptions, we conclude by offering a cause for hope that this transformation can be brought about: the recent demise of the MAI. The failure of efforts to establish an international investor-rights agreement also reveals the power of arguments concerning the impacts of these global regimes on culture and the environment.

In the fall of 1998, the forward march of global free trade suffered a significant defeat when efforts to establish a Multilateral Agreement on Investment (MAI) under the auspices of the Organization for Economic Cooperation and Development (OECD) had to be abandoned. At the pivotal moment, the government of France decided to withdraw from negotiations, and released a report explaining its reasons for doing so. Prominently featured were concerns about the impact of the MAI on its sovereign prerogatives to protect its culture and environment. France also explicitly acknowledged the critical role that civil society had played in exposing the impacts of the MAI.[112]

Indeed, the cultural and environmental critiques of the MAI were among the most powerful exposés of the disastrous consequences of this international treaty. While the deregulation of financial services or the airline and telecommunications industries may seem arcane to many, virtually everyone understands the critical role of governments, law, and regulation in protecting the environment and preserving cultural diversity.

There are other reasons to regard the defeat of the MAI as a turning point in what has been thus far a headlong and largely unguided rush into globalization.[113] Many of the consequences of the "leap of faith" into free trade accomplished by the WTO and other trade agreements are now becoming painfully apparent in both developed and developing countries. This has led to a much broader and more sophisticated understanding of the impacts of this global agenda than existed a scant five years ago when the WTO was created.

The challenge now will be to ensure that further progress of the free trade agenda is halted until there has been an honest assessment of its impacts. As this guide illustrates, any objective appraisal soon reveals the need for the most fundamental reforms to current trade policies. Because if left unchanged, these policies will propel us along a course that can only lead—socially, economically, and environmentally—to a dead end.

Endnotes

1. World Commission on Environment and Development (WCED), Gro Harlem Brundtlan, chair: *Our Common Future* (Oxford University Press 1987), p.3. (herein referred to as "Brundtland")
2. Brundtland, supra 1, p.84.
3. "Democracy, transparency don't exist at WTO;" International Press Service, K. Senevirtane, reporting an interview with Walden Bellow and others at the conclusion of the WTO Ministerial meeting in Singapore in Dec. 1996.
4. See, for example, Robert Reich, *The Work of Nations: Preparing Ourselves for the 21st Century Capitalism*, p. 113 (1992).
5. See "Reformulated Gasoline" case note in Chapter 8.
6. The Federal Minister for International Trade in response to a question posed on the House of Commons Order Paper. See Frank Tester, "Free Trading the Environment," in Duncan Cameron, ed., *The Free Trade Deal* (Toronto: Lorimer and Company, 1988).
7. See discussion in Chapter 10 concerning the TRIPs Agreement.
8. See *The Results of the Uruguay Round of Multilateral Trade Negotiations: The Legal Texts*, reprinted by the WTO in 1995, ISBN 92-870-1124-4.
9. See *United States: Restrictions on Imports of Tuna*, GATT Doc. DS21/R, B.I.S.D. (39th Supp.) and *United States: Restrictions on the Imports of Tuna*, GATT Doc. DS/29R (June 1994), unadopted.
10. With the exceptions of Friends of the Earth, the Sierra Club, and Greenpeace, major U.S. environmental groups were willing to support the first major initiative of a newly elected president in return for these marginal reforms. In Canada, environmental groups were almost unanimous in their opposition.
11. Canadian Conference of the Arts, *At Home in the World: An International Forum on Culture and Cooperation*, a statement endorsed by more than 170 people representing over 60 non-governmental organizations in the arts, culture and development from Canada and other nations, in Ottawa, on June 29, 1998.

12. For an excellent discussion of the importance of diversity to our survival, see David Suzuki, *The Sacred Balance: Rediscovering our Place in Nature* (Toronto: Greystone Books, 1996).

13. These statistics are taken from a speech presented by Victor Rabinovich (at the time, the Assistant Deputy Minister for Cultural Development and Heritage at the Department of Canadian Heritage) "The Social and Economic Rationales for Canada's Domestic Cultural Programs," in *The Culture and Free Trade Quandary*, Ed. Dennis Browne, the Centre for Trade Policy and Law, University of Ottawa, 1998.

14. Benjamin R. Barber, *Jihad vs. McWorld* (Random House of Canada Ltd., 1995) p. 92.

15. Ibid.

16. Bernard Ostry, *Culture and Trade: One Policy/No Options*, supra note 13, p. 19.

17. Supra note 14, pp. 97–98.

18. See "Barshevsky Reveals U.S. Push to Broaden WTO Services Talks," *Inside U.S. Trade* Vol. 17, No. 22 (June 4, 1999).

19. Support for this view can be found in a report by the U.S. General Accounting Office which describes NAFTA Annex 2106 as "the agreement's automatic retaliation provision...." See U.S. GAO, *North American Free Trade Agreement: Assessment of Major Issues 2* (Sept. 1993) p. 100 (GAO/ ggd-93–137).

20. Ted Magder, "Franchising the Candy Store: Split-Run Magazines and a New International Regime for Trade in Culture," *Canadian-American Public Policy*, the Canadian-American Center, the University of Maine, Number 34 (April 1998) p. 49.

21. Ibid, p. 7.

22. Ibid, pp. 27–28.

23. Ibid.

24. The abandonment by Canada of its authority to use tariffs to protect Canadian culture can actually be found in the cultural "exemption" provision of the FTA, which specifically indicates that tariff reduction commitments of the free trade agreement apply to cultural products.

25. *Canada: Certain Measures Concerning Periodicals*, Report of the Appellate Body (June 30, 1997). WT/DS31/AB/R.

26. The case also involved a successful challenge to differential postal rates that effectively provided a subsidy to domestic magazines.

27. *Maclean's*, "Raising the Stakes Over Magazines: Washington Threatens Trade War" (Jan. 25, 1999).

28. *United States: Malt Beverages*, adopted; 19 June 1992, BISD 39S/206, *Japan: Alcoholic Beverages*; adopted Nov. 1, 1996, WT/DS11/AB/R.

29. *Maclean's*, "Mad About Magazines" (May 10, 1999).

30. See *Report on the Multilateral Agreement on Investment (MAI)* (September 1998), Catherine Lalumière, Member of the European Parliament; and Jean-Pierre Landau, Inspector General, Finance.

31. Lehman and Krebs, "Control of the World's Food Supply," *The Case Against the Global Economy* (San Francisco: Sierra Club Books, 1996).

32. United Nations, Food and International Trade: World Food Summit (1996) TECH, Section 3.28.

33. Goldin Knudsen and van der Mensbrugghe, "Trade Liberalisation: Global Economic Implications," OECD/World Bank (Paris 1993).

34. Mark Ritchie, "Reflections on the World Food Summit," The Institute for Agriculture and Trade Policy (Dec. 1996).

35. "GATT and Third World Agriculture," *The Ecologist*, Vol.23, No.6 (Nov/Dec 1993).

36. See Agriculture, Chapter 4.

37. *United States: Import Prohibition of Certain Shrimp and Shrimp Products.*

38. *Canada: Measures Affecting Exports of Unprocessed Herring and Salmon*, L/6268, adopted March 1988, 35S/98, and *In the Matter of Canada's Landing Requirement for Pacific Coast Salmon and Herring*, October 16, 1989.

39. "The Freshwater Resources of the World: A Comprehensive Assessment," report of the Secretary General of the United Nations, February 1997.

40. Ibid.

41. "National Water Crisis Forecast," *Globe and Mail*, June 7, 2000.

42. The Boundary Waters Treaty Act is a bilateral agreement between Canada and the United States concerning the Great Lakes and certain specified international water courses.

43. "Options Paper for Canadian Council of Ministers of the Environment, discussing various options for the Minister's CCME meeting," May 19–20, 1999. See discussion of International Trade Considerations.

44. See Sporhase *v.* Nebraska, 458 U.S. 941 (1982); and City of El Paso *v.* Reynolds, 563 F. Supp. 379 (D.N.M. 1983).

45. "Report to the Council of Great Lakes Governors: Governing the Withdrawal of Water from the Great Lakes," Lochead et al., May 18, 1999.

46. See Commission *v.* Italy, (Case 7/68) and Commission *v.* Ireland Re Dundalk Water Supply (Case 45/87).

47. In British Columbia, for example, as of 1993 approximately 40,000 licenses for the withdrawal of surface water were in existence in the province, and many provincial water sources are identified by the BC Ministry of Environment as being overtaxed. In the Great Lakes, the largest single use of water is for the very commercial purpose of generating hydroelectric power and is estimated to exceed one trillion gallons per day. In Ontario, millions of litres of water are withdrawn from groundwater aquifers by commercial water bottling companies each day.

48. See "NAFTA and Water Exports," the Canadian Environmental Law Association, 1993, and references cited therein.

49. See press statement issued by the Office of the United States Trade Representative, December 2, 1993. Referring to the 1993 statement and others, the USTR states: "None of these statements change the NAFTA in any way."

50. For a further discussion of the investment and services disciplines of these trade agreements see Chapters 11 and 12.

51. See the statement issued by the Department of Foreign Affairs and International Trade on April 7, 1999.

52. Metalclad vs. Mexico is the first investor–state claim to find in favour of a foreign investor. In this case, a hazardous waste disposal company proceeded to build a disposal facility near a Mexican community, notwithstanding vigorous local resistance. When the community got an injunction to prevent the facility from operating, the company sued under NAFTA investment rules. The fact that the company never bothered to apply for a local construction permit before starting its project

didn't discourage the international tribunal from finding in its favour. The investment provisions of NAFTA are discussed in more detail in Chapter 11.

53. Under NAFTA Article 104 and Annex 104, certain international and bilateral agreements are accorded certain protections from the full application of trade disciplines—the BWTA is not listed among them.

54. NAFTA Article 605.

55. Ibid.

56. See discussion of this and other basic GATT rules in Chapter 2.

57. NAFTA Article 608.2.

58. See Arden-Clark, "Environmental Taxes and Charges and Border Tax Adjustment," *GATT Rules and Energy Taxes*, World Wildlife Fund for Nature, Gland Switzerland, 1994.

59. The Working Party on "Border Tax Adjustments" 1968–1970.

60. See Article 2.2 of the TBT Agreement.

61. Johnathan Dahl, "Perilous Policy: Canada Promotes Asbestos Mining, Sells Carcinogenic Mineral Heavily in Third World," *Wall Street Journal*, Dec. 9, 1989.

62. André Picard and Harvey Enchin, "Quebec planning to fight US asbestos ban," *Globe and Mail, Report on Business*, July 7, 1989.

63. Ibid.

64. Mines Minister Raymond Savoie, supra note 47.

65. "French asbestos ban blow to Quebec: Chain reaction in other countries feared," *Globe and Mail*, July 4, 1996.

66. "Government of Canada Stepping up Action to Fight French Asbestos Ban, McLellan and Eggleton say," Natural Resources Canada and Foreign Affairs and International Trade, October 8, 1996.

67. *United States: Standards for Reformulated and Conventional Gasoline*, WTO Doc. WT/DSR/R (Jan. 29, 1996), 35 I.L.M. 274.

68. The Gasoline Rule prohibited the sale of conventional gasoline in these areas and mandated a 15% reduction in VOC and Nox emissions from reformulated gasoline products, as measured against a 1990 baseline year. For conventional gasoline sold elsewhere, levels of contaminants needed to be held at levels no worse than 1990 baseline levels.

69. "The Auto Pact's demise would be welcome news," *Globe and Mail*, editorial page, July 13, 1999.

70. Daly and Cobb, *For the Common Good* (Boston: Beacon Press, 1989) pp. 209–215.

71. Ibid, pp. 213–215.

72. See discussion in Chapter 6 concerning the use of export controls and tariffs to support domestic value-added investment for natural resource dependent local and regional economies.

73. *Canada: Measures Affecting the Export of Civilian Aircraft.*

74. Canadian Press, "Ottawa says it wins trade dispute with Brazil," March 12, 1999.

75. "Brashefsky Reveals U.S. Push to Broaden WTO Services Talks," *Inside U.S. Trade*, Vol. 17, No. 22, June 4, 1999.

76. The General Agreement on Investment Measures (TRIMs), currently one of the WTO Agreements, represents only a rudimentary framework for the disciplines that have been established by several bilateral investment agreements and NAFTA. See discussion in Chapter 11.

77. "Japan Takes First Step Toward WTO Challenge of Canada Auto Pact," *Inside US Trade*, July 10, 1998.

78. *Alternatives for Americas: Building a People's Hemispheric Agreement*, the Canadian Centre for Policy Alternatives and Common Frontiers, 1999.

79. Ibid.

80. Submission by the Canadian Labour Congress to the House of Commons Standing Committee on Foreign Affairs and International Trade, Regarding Pending World Trade Organization (WTO) Negotiations, April 27, 1999.

81. Agreement on Trade-Related Aspects of Intellectual Property Rights, Article 27.

82. Vandana Shiva and Radha Holla-Bhar, "Piracy by Patent: The Case of the Neem Tree," *The Case Against the Global Economy*, Ed. Jerry Mander and Edward Goldsmith (San Francisco: Sierra Club Books, 1996).

83. Aaron Cosbey, *The Sustainable Development Effects of the WTO Trips Agreement: A Focus on Developing Countries*, the International Institute for Sustainable Development, Feb. 1997.

84. See, for example, the Convention on Biological Diversity (1992) Article 16: Access to and Transfer of Technology.

85. Laura Eggerton, "Ministers Reject use of Loopholes to Cut Drug Patents," *Globe and Mail*, Mar. 6, 1997.

86. See proceedings of the federal Standing Committee on the Environment and Sustainable Development, Feb. 3, 1998.

87. This is made explicit in annotations to the Oct. '97 draft text of the MAI. See Article II 2. (vii) and p. 102.

88. Before withdrawing from negotiations, France described the combined effect of MAI provisions as "explosive" and as creating a dual dissymmetry by favouring the rights of corporations over those of nations and by favouring foreign over national investors. See Lalumiere and Landau, & quot; Report on the Multilateral Agreement on Investment (MAI) & quot; published by France's Ministry of the Economy, Finance and Industry, supra note 30.

89. While representatives of the federal government have promoted these agreements as doing no more than assuring foreign investors equal treatment under Canadian law, even those who are in favour of the MAI agree that this is not the case. On this point, members of the international trade bar are unanimous; see the proceedings of British Columbia Special Legislative Committee on the MAI on September 30, 1998, and the evidence of Professor Bob Paterson of the UBC Law School, Milos Barutciski LLB of Davies, Ward and Beck, Barry Appleton LLB, of Appleton and Associates, and Steven Shrybman, LLB, of the West Coast Environmental Law Association.

90. "Ethyl sues Canada over MMT law," *Globe and Mail*, April 15, 1997.

91. See editorials in the *Financial Post*, "Why the secrecy over investor rights?" Aug. 29–31, 1998, and in the *Globe and Mail*, "Can we talk," Sept 10, 1998.

92. See evidence of Barry Appleton, Steven Shrybman, and Prof. Bob Patterson, supra note 75.

93. See supra note 74.

94. Sinclair, *GATS: How the World Trade Organization's new "services" negotiations theaten democracy*. CCPA, 2000.

95. The Canadian Centre for Policy Alternatives: *The Future of Medicare: Recovering the Canada Health Act,* September 1999 ISBN: 0-88627-1487.

96. These are listed under NAFTA Annexes I and II.

97. This expectation is captured by the principles of standstill and rollback. Standstill precludes the development of law and policy that would be more restrictive of the rights established by the treaty, and the principle of rollback anticipates the gradual reduction of the protection afforded by particular reservations.

98. *Annex II C-9.*

99. Letter of Nov. 26, 1999 to the Honourable Halvar Jonson from the federal Minister of Health.

100. See WTO disputes concerning Canada's Auto Pact: CANADA – CERTAIN MEASURES AFFECTING THE AUTOMOTIVE INDUSTRY, AB-2000-2; and Europe's preferential tariff treatment of bananas imported from certain former colonies under the Lome Convention: EUROPEAN COMMUNITIES—REGIME FOR THE IMPORTATION, SALE AND DISTRIBUTION OF BANANAS/AB 1997-3.

   In the Auto Pact case Canada conceded to the WTO tribunal that it had made an error in listing auto sales under the wrong heading of the United Nations Central Products Code, which provides the framework Canada is using to list its commitments. In the Periodicals case Canada mistakenly believed that because it had not listed advertising that it was on safe terrain in establishing measures to protect Canadian publishers from unfair US competition.

101. Ibid.

102. Trebilcock and Howse, *The Regulation of International Trade,* Routledge, p. 220.

103. Unless this boast has been removed, it can be found on the GATS homepage on the WTO internet site.

104. See for example: WTO, Environmental Services: Background Note by the Secretariat, July 6, 1998. S/C/W/46

105. A similar provision of NAFTA is being used by UPS, the US courier company, to support a hundred $million investor–state claim against Canada concerning Canadian postal services. UPS argues that Canada Post is taking advantage of its monopoly mail delivery infrastructure to support competitive parcel and courier services. The same challenge might just as readily be made with respect to the use of public hospitals to deliver services that are also offered by private clinics.

106. Supra note 9, p. 219.

107. For example, under Canada's Schedule of Specific Commitments, subsidies to public sector services are reserved from National Treatment obligations. Also reserved are measures "related to the supply of services required to be offered to the public generally," public education, social welfare, and health are noted. See GATS/SC/16, pp. 3–5.

108. "Ottawa to spend $1–billion on Internet initiative," *Globe and Mail*, Oct. 17, 2000.

109. Annex on Financial Services, Section 1. Scope and Definition subsection (b)(iii).

110. Benjamine R. Barber, *Jihad vs. McWorld* (Random House of Canada Ltd., 1995).

111. Personal communication with the European Ambassador to GATT Negotiations, Tran Van Tanh, during an informal round-table discussion at a meeting convened by the Institute for Agriculture and the Environment in Amsterdam in 1992. Mr. Van Tanh candidly described GATT negotiations as "anti-democratic, not un-democratic."

112. Supra note 30.

113. In the U.S. Congress "fast-track" authorization has been defeated twice during recent years in spite of determined efforts by the executive and large corporations to get approval. Fast track rules suspend the prerogatives of Congress to amend the legislation implementing international trade agreements. Without it, other countries are simply unwilling to negotiate with the U.S., knowing that the fruits of those negotiations may be undone by Congress.